PEARL HARBOR

THE DAY OF INFAMY — AN ILLUSTRATED HISTORY

PEARL HARBOR

THE DAY OF INFAMY — AN ILLUSTRATED HISTORY

BY DAN VAN DER VAT

Introduction by SENATOR JOHN McCAIN Paintings by TOM FREEMAN

Historical Consultant: John Lundstrom

CHARTWELL
BOOKS, INC.

A CHARTWELL BOOKS/MADISON PRESS BOOK

This edition published in 2007 by

CHARTWELL BOOKS,
A Division of
BOOK SALES, INC.
114 Northfield Avenue
Edison, New Jersey 08837
USA

ISBN-13: 978-0-7858-2352-0
ISBN-10: 0-7858-2352-2

Printed in China

(Page 1) A tattered American flag saved
from the USS *Shaw*.

(Pages 2–3) A rainbow illuminates the
Arizona Memorial in Pearl Harbor.

(Pages 4–5) The hills of Oahu's Waianae
Range, over which Japanese fighters
raced southward on December 7, 1941.

(Pages 6–7) Sailors place Hawaiian leis
on the graves of Pearl Harbor casualties
in 1945.

(Pages 8–9) A Japanese bomber over
Hickam Field during the attack.

"At the going down of the
sun and in the morning
We will remember them."

From "For the Fallen,"
by Laurence Binyon, 1914

Contents

Introduction

THE PAST FEW YEARS HAVE WITNESSED A RESURGENCE OF INTEREST in what has popularly been called the last great war. Films like *Saving Private Ryan* and books like Tom Brokaw's *The Greatest Generation* and James Bradley and Ron Powers' *Flags of Our Fathers* have played an instrumental role in reminding the public of a period that saw the United States mobilized toward a single purpose like at no other time in its history — the defeat of fascism in Europe and of Japanese hegemony in Asia.

The divisions in our society that existed in the period leading up to the Japanese attack on US forces at Pearl Harbor tend to be forgotten. Our collective memory appropriately takes pride in our achievements once mobilized for war. The book that follows, however, will serve as a reminder that the United States — the country that emerged from World War II the most powerful nation in history — entered the war unprepared and riven with internal divisions regarding our place in the world and a vision of where we wanted to go. It is an illustrated history. Its intention is to educate through narrative, pictorial history, and paintings inspired by the events discussed.

And those events changed the course of world history. The architect of Japan's bold stroke against American naval forces at Pearl Harbor, the respected Japanese Admiral Isoroku Yamamoto, harbored few illusions regarding the nature of the country he was ordered to attack. Well versed in American culture and industrial capacity, Admiral Yamamoto prophetically proclaimed, upon receiving word of his magnificent victory at Pearl Harbor: "We have awakened a sleeping giant and have instilled in him a terrible resolve." The admiral's eventual death at the hands of American fighter pilots constituted an exclamation mark on his fateful prediction. Galvanized as a nation, the American people responded with a war effort that would take them to victory in the Pacific even as Allied forces entered Berlin.

Both my grandfather and father fought in World War II. My grandfather stood on the deck of the USS *Missouri* in Tokyo Bay to witness the signing by the Japanese of the documents of surrender.

In between the events at Pearl Harbor and that moment aboard the *Missouri*, the world, and the United States in particular, underwent a monumental transformation. Vicious battles under the most terrible conditions were the norm in the Pacific Theater. From Bougainville to Corrigedor to Hiroshima, the United States avenged its humiliation and loss at Pearl Harbor with a tenacity and courage that should never be permitted to fade from our memory.

Ten years after the Persian Gulf War, I continue to marvel at the scale of that military victory and at the blessedly low number of American dead. It has become too easy to forget the sacrifices of an earlier generation in the struggle to rid the world of tyranny — a struggle manifest not just during World War II, but in Korea and Indochina as well. Nearly twenty-four hundred American servicemen were killed at Pearl Harbor, a tragic prelude to the tens of thousands more who would perish in places few knew existed the day before the first bombs fell on Battleship Row.

Off Ford Island in Hawaii is the memorial to the USS *Arizona*, a ship named for the state I am honored to represent in Congress. Parts of its structure emerge from the waters of the bay like a cast-iron headstone. The *Arizona* remains the final resting place for 1,177 of its crew. Sixty years after Japanese bombs sent it to its watery grave, it continues to stand as a silent testament to the sacrifice of so many in defense of liberty. It also serves to remind us of the need to remain vigilant.

Dan van der Vat's book is an important contribution to the literature about the events leading up to World War II and the Japanese attack on Pearl Harbor. He has performed an admirable service by combining concise yet insightful narrative with a wealth of photographs and paintings in telling the story of what President Roosevelt famously termed in the attack's aftermath, "a date which will live in infamy." With each visit to the USS *Arizona* Memorial, I am compelled to reflect again on the tragedy that befell the men and women who perished in the attack on Pearl Harbor, and on those who died thousands of miles from home in the war that followed. In the caption accompanying one of the photographs, van der Vat quotes an officer serving aboard the *Arizona* the day before the Japanese attack. "By this time next week," Captain Franklin Van Valkenburgh wrote, "we will be on our way home for Christmas." Nothing more need be said.

— *John McCain*

A Carpenter's Sacrifice

Shattered by six torpedoes in the opening minutes of the attack on Pearl Harbor on December 7, 1941, the 29,000-ton battleship USS *Oklahoma* began to capsize.

In the ship's dispensary, gurneys, glass cabinets, surgical instruments, and bottles flew through the air as twenty-five-year-old Ensign Adolph Mortensen thudded onto the ceiling, now under his feet.

The compartment quickly filled with water, except for an air pocket in one corner that Mortensen now shared with three other men. Stretching his foot underwater toward the ship's side, the young ensign located a porthole. It would be tight, barely wide enough even for a thin man. As an officer should, he ordered the three enlisted men to precede

(Above) Ensign Adolph Mortensen. (Right) Chief Carpenter John Arnold Austin. (Below) Rescuers atop the hull of the overturned *Oklahoma*.

him through the opening. Two obeyed as fast as they could.

The third, Chief Carpenter John Arnold Austin, refused. He weighed over two hundred pounds and knew he could not get out. A big man in every sense, he held the porthole open for the others. As Mortensen squeezed through, he lost the pajama bottoms he was wearing when the alarm sounded.

"As far as I can tell, I was the last man to escape from the ship without [outside] help," Mortensen recalled after the war. "[Austin's] was the most noble and heroic act a man could perform, knowing full well that his minutes were few."

For his sacrifice, John Austin was awarded a posthumous Navy Cross. He was just one of 2,390 Americans who died in the surprise air attack by the Japanese on the United States battlefleet in its heavily fortified main Pacific base. But his selfless courage in a ship and a world turned upside down was far from unique. On dozens of ships, and ashore and in the air, brave individuals had already begun to fight back. Ultimately, their courage and spirit would turn America's worst military disaster into her greatest triumph.

The Path to War

At the end of the nineteenth century, "manifest destiny" led the United States beyond the west coast of its own continent across the Pacific toward China. At the same time, a reviving Japanese Empire was expanding on the other side of that ocean. From the early years of the twentieth century, a clash between these two vigorous powers, both new to the world stage, seemed only a matter of time — even to contemporary observers.

These are some of the events that set the stage for the war in the Pacific in 1941.

1868
Shogun rule is overthrown and Emperor Mutsuhito re-establishes the supremacy of the throne. With his "Meiji Revolution," Japan embraces western ideas, institutions, and technologies.

1878
An Army general staff that is outside democratic, parliamentary control is set up in Japan — allowing the Emperor's generals to function independently.

1895
Japan defeats China in Korea after a surprise attack.

1898
The United States annexes Hawaii, Guam, and Wake Island as stepping-stones across the Pacific and wrests the Philippines from Spain.

| 1850 | 1855 | 1860 | 1865 | 1870 | 1875 | 1880 | 1885 | 1890 | 1895 |

1853–54
A US naval squadron, led by Commodore Matthew Perry, forces Japan to open some ports to American shipping, ending centuries of isolation.

1858
All Japanese ports are thrown open to western trade.

1889
The Japanese constitution is westernized as the Empire decides to acquire the key symbols of world status: a battlefleet and overseas territories.

1902
Japan concludes its alliance with the United Kingdom.

1904–05
Japan defeats Tsarist Russia — on land in northern China, and at sea with a crushing naval victory at the Battle of Tsushima. The war starts with a signature surprise attack by the Japanese.

1921

Japan seeks to monopolize influence over China as US trade interests grow. America favors an "Open Door" policy in China.

1922

The Washington Conference, an initiative by US President Warren Harding, produces a nine-nation treaty on China and also limits the size of the world's five leading fleets. The US and Japan sign both pacts.

1910

Japan formally annexes Korea.

1914–18

Against the backdrop of the Great War in Europe, Japan — as Britain's ally — seizes German possessions in China and the Pacific, keeping many as "mandates" after the war.

1936

Japan signs the Anti-Comintern Pact with Germany, agreeing not to support the Soviet Union if Germany wages war against it.

- The Japanese Fleet undergoes massive expansion.
- Tension in Tokyo builds over whether to expand northward at the expense of the Soviet Union — or southward, against Europe's Asian colonies.

1937

Japan concocts a "China Incident," provoking a new war and tying down huge armies without hope of decisive victory.

- In a major speech in Chicago, President Roosevelt calls for a "quarantine" of Japanese "lawlessness."
- On December 13, the American gunboat USS *Panay* is sunk by Japanese aircraft in China's Yangtze River while escorting American oil tankers.

1940

In May, Pearl Harbor becomes the main Pacific base of the United States Fleet.

- Japan abandons its northern strategy in favor of southward expansion and proclaims the Great East Asia Co-Prosperity Sphere.
- The US slaps an embargo on metal exports to Japan.
- Tokyo concludes the Tripartite ("Axis") Pact with Germany and Italy.
- The British cripple the Italian battlefleet in a raid on Taranto harbor.

| 1905 | 1910 | 1915 | 1920 | 1925 | 1930 | 1935 | 1940 | 1945 |

1918

Japan starts to use Korea as a springboard for ousting the Russians and Chinese from Manchuria.

1931

Japan concocts "an incident" as an excuse to conquer Manchuria and converts it into the puppet empire of Manchukuo.

1933

Condemned by the League of Nations for its aggression in Manchuria, Japan walks out of the organization.

- Hitler takes power in Germany.
- Army and Navy staffs dominate the government in Tokyo.

1938

- Japan closes America's "Open Door" in China and Manchuria and announces a "New Order in East Asia."
- Roosevelt calls for a "moral embargo" of Japan.

1939

- The Soviet Union drives Japanese intruders back into Manchuria after heavy border fighting. Tokyo's "northern option" appears doomed.
- America renounces its trade treaty with Japan.
- Hitler signs a non-aggression pact with Stalin and goes to war in Europe.

1941

In April, Japan concludes a neutrality pact with the Soviet Union and in summer moves troops and planes into French Indochina in readiness for southward expansion.

- In June, Germany invades the Soviet Union.
- In July, America places an embargo on all strategic exports to Japan, and freezes Japan's assets in the US.
- Diplomatic peace efforts in Washington and Tokyo reach a stand-off, but talks are set to resume — on December 7.

Part One **WILL THERE BE WAR?**

CHAPTER ONE

Operation "Hawaii"

"Admiral Onishi requested me to draw up a plan for a possible attack [on Pearl Harbor]. I made an investigation and concluded the attack was difficult but possible."

— Captain Minoru Genda, Imperial Japanese Navy

A RAID ON PEARL HARBOR WAS SEEN AS EQUALLY LIKELY IN BOTH THE UNITED STATES AND Japan in the event of war between the two countries. A British journalist explored the idea as early as 1925, and a Japanese naval pilot drafted a plan in 1927. It featured, though tentatively, for years in the Japanese naval staff's war games. And in the early 1930s, the US Navy itself proved its viability when American carriers, including the USS *Lexington* under the command of Captain Ernest J. King, the future wartime naval chief, launched a spectacular, surprise "air raid" on the base.

Three events in 1940 helped turn the idea into the keystone of Japanese strategy. In May, the US Navy made Pearl Harbor its main Pacific base. At about the same time, Admiral Isoroku Yamamoto, commander in chief of the Japanese Combined Fleet since August 30, 1939, began to think aloud about raiding Pearl Harbor. The diminutive admiral, then fifty-six, was an incorrigible gambler who had learned to play poker at Harvard and while he was a naval attaché in Washington. Although his service led the world in naval aviation by 1940, the idea of raiding Hawaii as an adjunct to the southern strategy might have remained a pipe dream but for the third event.

On November 11, a single British carrier, HMS *Illustrious,* launched just twenty-one obsolete Swordfish biplanes in an unprecedented torpedo attack on Mussolini's battle-fleet in its heavily protected main base at Taranto, Italy. Seven vessels, including three battleships, were crippled in the dashing, low-level raid over the shallow water of the port. Just two British planes were lost, and the balance of power in the Mediterranean was shifted toward the Royal Navy for six months.

A Japanese assistant naval attaché flew from Berlin to Taranto to analyze the effect of

(Left) Pearl Harbor was named *Wai Momi* or "Pearl Waters" by the Hawaiians for the pearl oysters that once thrived there. Today, it looks much as it did in 1941 (right), still dominated by Ford Island with its large naval air station — although a causeway now links the island to the mainland.

(Pages 16–17) USS *Arizona* moves into its mooring on Battleship Row on Saturday morning, December 6, 1941.

The Raid on Taranto

From the naval base at Taranto (top) at the southern tip of the boot of Italy, Mussolini's fleet could easily menace British convoys bound for beleaguered Malta and the Middle East. In a daring night raid on November 11, 1940, British carrier planes knocked out three battleships there, including the powerful *Conte di Cavour* (above). The success of this mission encouraged the Japanese to consider a surprise attack on Pearl Harbor.

the attack and report back to the highest levels of the Japanese naval command. He saw that not only had the British achieved complete tactical surprise but they had also overcome the main challenge of the operation: preventing torpedoes launched by aircraft from burying themselves in the bottom of a shallow anchorage. If a handful of biplanes could achieve so much, imagine what a massed attack by Japan's ultra-modern maritime aircraft could do to the American battlefleet in its shallow main base.

✪

ONCE YAMAMOTO CONCLUDED THAT WAR WITH BRITAIN AND America was inevitable, he decided it was essential to knock out the only force capable of seriously obstructing, if not halting, Japan — the United States Pacific Fleet. Until January 1941, the Imperial Navy's strategy was defensive, envisaging a "great decisive battle" near Japan — a new Tsushima. Yamamoto, however, favored an aggressive strategy: instead of waiting for the Americans to come to them, the Japanese would copy Hitler and his apparently all-conquering *Blitzkrieg* (lightning war). The aim now was to establish a perimeter as far into the Indian and Pacific oceans as practicable by an intricately coordinated, multiple surprise attack. Then the Empire could consolidate with impunity — provided the US fleet (and the American Philippines) were neutralized simultaneously at the outset. When — if — the Americans recovered from the preemptive strike, they would face a *fait accompli,* with Japan in an unassailable position.

Yamamoto worked up his carrier forces in 1940–41, making them the best in the world. On January 7, 1941, in a long and passionate letter to Admiral Koshiro Oikawa, the Navy minister, he pressed the case for making the strike on Hawaii an integral part of the southward advance. But Yamamoto had already asked Rear Admiral Takijiro Onishi, chief of staff of the Eleventh Air Fleet, to explore the idea, telling his Combined Fleet chief of staff, Rear Admiral Shigeru Fukudome, in December 1940:

> *I want to have Onishi study a Pearl Harbor attack plan as a tentative step. After studying the result of his report, the problem may be included in the fleet training program, and I want to keep it secret until that time.*

Yamamoto won over the ministry to Operation "Hawaii" by sheer force of personality; we can be sure the hawks were delighted. Astonishingly, a rumor that Japan intended to bomb Pearl

Harbor was circulating in Tokyo within weeks of the Navy Ministry's decision to include the idea in its war plans. The American ambassador, Joseph C. Grew, an old Japan hand, picked it up on January 27 from an unexpected source: the head of the Peruvian Legation, Minister Ricardo Rivera-Schreiber.

> *My Peruvian colleague told a member of my staff that he had heard from many sources that the Japanese military forces planned, in the event of trouble with the United States, to attempt a surprise mass attack on Pearl Harbor. Although the project seemed fantastic, the fact that he had heard it from many sources prompted him to pass [it] on.*

It was forwarded by naval intelligence in Washington to Admiral Husband E. Kimmel at Pearl Harbor. No American official took the rumor seriously (any more than Grew did: he was surely just covering himself), or tried to find out whether it was true, or just another straw in the wind in the fraught year of 1941.

✪

> *In February 1941, at the order of Admiral Yamamoto, Admiral Onishi requested me to draw up a plan for a possible attack. I made an investigation and concluded the attack was difficult but possible: I thought the best plan was to attack by planes but not to land. In June and July, I began to check on the details. The carrier pilots' crews [sic] were trained for the attack beginning in September and going intensively into training in October.*

SUCH WAS THE GENESIS OF OPERATION "HAWAII," ALSO CODENAMED "Z," as told by Captain Minoru Genda to his American interrogators in 1945. The difficulties to which he referred were daunting indeed. Pearl Harbor's depth, a scant forty feet, made using aircraft-launched torpedoes difficult. Even when launched at masthead level, they tended to run deep, often diving one hundred feet or more before rising to the surface. The battleships also boasted armored decks that normal bombs, dropped from high altitude, couldn't penetrate. Then there were the predictably heavy defenses of the great base, including fighters, antiaircraft guns afloat and ashore, radar, bomb shelters, and patrolling guard ships.

Genda, a commander early in 1941, was an aviation staff officer. Born in 1904, he qualified at the top of his year as a naval pilot in 1929 and came to fame as leader of "Genda's Flying Circus" of stunt pilots. He became an instructor and was also a

Admiral Isoroku Yamamoto, Commander in Chief of the Japanese Combined Fleet

Though Isoroku Yamamoto never earned a pilot's wings, he astutely chose to specialize in naval aviation as he rose through the ranks. Born at Nagaoka in 1884, the son of a former samurai, Yamamoto received his baptism of fire at the Battle of Tsushima in 1905. Much admired as a professional, he was also much hated by the expansionist hawks for his considered opposition to military adventurism. Although he enjoyed Japanese chess (*shogi*), Chinese mah-jongg and American poker, as a gambler he preferred calculated risks. Ironically, powerful friends among Japan's doves secured his elevation to commander in chief of the Combined Fleet. Fearing he might fall victim to some fanatic zealot — a not uncommon occurrence in 1930s Japan — they reasoned that he would be safest among the 40,000 sailors of Japan's highest seagoing command. Promoted to full admiral in 1940, he was opposed to war in general and with the United States in particular. However, as a professional, he believed that if war came it should be waged to the utmost.

Kido Butai — The Carrier Striking Force

The Japanese striking force assembled for the surprise attack on Pearl Harbor was the single largest carrier group that had ever taken to the seas. Never before had six aircraft carriers and their supporting ships entered combat as a combined fleet under one command. And never before had an attacking force adopted the strategy of delivering its offensive punch entirely by air. The success of the mission depended on the rigorously trained airmen of Japan's naval air fleet and on three types of airplane: the Kate torpedo bomber (below and right, top), the speedy Zero (below, middle, and right bottom), and the Val dive-bomber (bottom). The carriers launched a total of 350 airplanes against their unsuspecting target.

Both the fliers and their aircraft had proved their worth during Japan's war with China. By December 1941, Japan possessed the best-trained naval air force in the world. Its Combined Fleet outnumbered and outgunned the American Pacific Fleet in every category except battleships. Strangely, however, the Americans underestimated Japan's naval air capability, just one of many errors of prewar complacency. By the time the war in the Pacific began, Japanese naval strategy had shifted from defending the western Pacific to going on the attack. This offensive doctrine was born of necessity. For Japan to prevail against the United States, it needed to strike early and win decisively. The Pearl Harbor striking force represents the ultimate realization of this offensive attitude. As time would tell, it would also prove by far its most effective.

Kate Torpedo Bomber

Zero Fighter

Val Dive-bomber

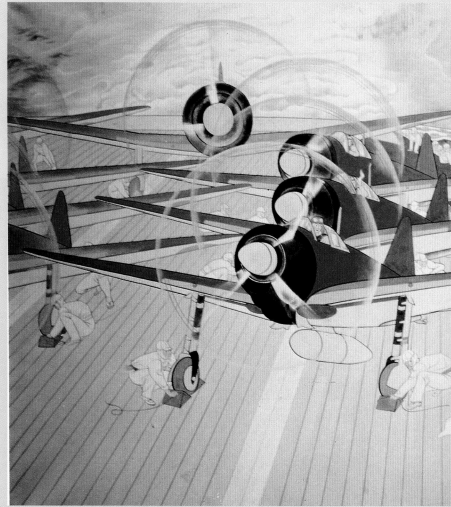

(Below) An artistic rendering of Japanese attack planes aboard one of the carriers.

profound thinker on strategy and tactics. He was known in the Navy as "Mad Genda," a revealing tag when fanaticism was quite normal in the Japanese officer corps.

Genda not only oversaw pilot training in the Mobile Force (*Kido Butai*) assembled against Hawaii but also overcame the formidable technical difficulties of torpedo attack in shallow, constricted waters. Fortunately for him, Japan boasted the world's best torpedoes, which proved adaptable to the highly specialized task. The answer to the tendency of the torpedoes to run deep was to attach extra wooden fins to them. The solution to armored decks was to fit steel fins to 16-inch, armor-piercing shells originally made for the main guns of battleships — creating bombs that struck point first.

Genda's bomber crews also adapted a tight flying formation. Once over their target, they practised dropping their bombs simultaneously, concentrating their weapons' destructive power. The need for more precise bombing was met by dive-bombers, while fighters would take on American planes and strafe ground targets. Intense training continued at various secluded bases in Japan until the very eve of the departure of the carriers to their assembly point in the Kurile Islands late in November 1941.

✪

HAVING MOVED THEIR FLEET TO OAHU IN MAY 1940 TO DETER JAPANESE AGGRESSION, THE Americans turned the island into the nation's, and purportedly the world's, strongest military outpost. Pearl Harbor was head and heart of the defenses; the large US Army presence of 45,000 was there specifically to protect the fleet and the air bases from attack by land or air or sabotage. American strategists realized that the fortress of Oahu faced four threats. In ascending order of likelihood they were: an invasion, a fleet action, a submarine attack, and an air raid from carriers.

The Territory of Hawaii had a population of about 460,000 in 1941, about one third of today's. One in three was ethnic Japanese, by far the largest element in a varied demographic stock that also included just 65,000 indigenous Hawaiians and 112,000 Caucasians. Then, as now, Oahu, though not by any means the largest, was the most heavily populated island, with about 275,000 people — overwhelmingly concentrated along the southern coastline in and around Pearl Harbor, Honolulu, and the beach resort of Waikiki.

Thanks to the military and naval buildup, Oahu was enjoying a building and employment boom in 1940 and 1941. More money per head of population was being invested in new construction in Honolulu in 1941 than in any other American city. The number of service personnel and their families was rapidly increasing and many thousands of civilians were also coming to live and work in Oahu. With Europe off limits to tourism, the number of visitors to the already famous Waikiki jumped by a quarter to a record 32,000 in 1941. And business was also booming along Hotel Street, home to dozens of garishly neon-lit bars catering to the island's soldiers, sailors, and marines.

"Motor traffic is almost unmanageable," the Hawaiian illustrated monthly, *Paradise of the Pacific*, reported in 1941. "It snarls wildly at times. Traffic accidents are the rule and not the exception. The number of traffic mortalities is appalling." Crime was on the increase, prostitution was a major problem, and there was a water shortage. With the demand for

A Citadel in Paradise

Oahu in 1941 was perhaps the most heavily garrisoned island in the world. But Waikiki Beach (above) drew a record number of tourists that year, and the sight of American bombers flying in formation over Diamond Head was likely an added attraction. For the thousands of servicemen stationed there, Hawaii only seemed like a South Seas paradise when they had time off. Visits to the islands' scenic wonders (middle right) were described in the many postcards (bottom right) sent stateside. (Top right) Reservists from the mainland board a naval craft that will take them to Pearl Harbor.

Sunset at Waikiki, Honolulu, T. H.

SURF RIDING, HAWAII.

traditional crops such as sugarcane (vanished today) and pineapples skyrocketing, the sleepy days of the years after the First World War were long gone. "We are living in an era of stress. The days ahead will be busy days — and some of them will be cloudy. If war comes, however, the islands will do their stint. All in all, the good year 1941 has been just that — a good year." So said the editorial in *Paradise of the Pacific* in its December 1941 issue — published in late November.

"Here in Hawaii," said the American Army commander, Walter C. Short, "we all live in a citadel. . . ." Oahu seemed a veritable hornet's nest, bristling with massive coastal guns, barracks, Army fighters, bombers and scouts, Marine Corps planes, and carrier- and land-based naval aircraft. But many of the Army machines were unserviceable, there was a serious shortage of reconnaissance planes, and antiaircraft guns and radar were sparse and undermanned. And although the two commanders, Admiral Husband E. Kimmel of the Pacific Fleet and General Short, got along well on a personal level, interservice coordination and cooperation were rudimentary at best.

✪

AMERICAN INTELLIGENCE SERVICES WERE MORE USED TO COOPeration. They had made major inroads into Japanese ciphers, with the Army attacking consular and then diplomatic traffic (the results were codenamed RED MAGIC and PURPLE MAGIC respectively), helped by the Navy, which also tackled Japanese naval signals. Both services operated interception stations around the Pacific rim; they also compared notes with British, Australian, and Dutch East Indies army codebreakers from well before the start of hostilities. The result was an imposing flood of raw information, but no individual or agency had a complete overview of it — a serious flaw that led to misinformation and missed information alike. Further, the Navy did not break the new Japanese cipher, JN-25, until after it went to war.

Insufficient attention was paid in particular to messages between the Japanese consulate general in Honolulu and the Foreign Ministry in Tokyo, traffic usually conducted in a lower-grade cipher and therefore given a low priority by the Americans. But the consulate, with its swollen staff of two hundred, was the main center of Japanese espionage on Oahu. The Japanese Navy sent a specially trained spy to Honolulu — Lieutenant Takeo Yoshikawa, aged twenty-nine, alias Tadashi Morimura, a consular

Should the Attack Have Been a Surprise?

Allied codebreakers — led by Commander Joseph J. Rochefort (below) at Pearl Harbor's Station Hypo (above) — did not decipher the Japanese naval code (JN-25) until March and April 1942, well after the start of the war. Had they done so in the fall of 1941, American intelligence would likely have been able to piece together the probability that Pearl Harbor would be the first target. But in the days before the attack, the Americans only knew that something big was afoot. This they could infer from reading the Japanese consular and diplomatic cipher, codenamed MAGIC. The joint Army/Navy intelligence office in Washington had constructed a machine that could decode diplomatic messages to and from the Japanese Embassy in Washington, but these messages contained no direct reference to an impending military operation.

The first solid hint that war was in the offing came on December 1, when a number of Japanese embassies and consulates received orders to destroy their cipher machines. However, it was only on the eve of the attack, December 6 — as intelligence officers in Washington began decrypting a fourteen-part message sent by Japan to its ambassador — that the Americans possessed strong evidence an attack was imminent. Somewhere. Allied intelligence had also been tracking a large Japanese convoy, obviously bound for Malaya, but without carrier escort.

In early December, the main job of Pearl Harbor's Station Hypo was listening to and locating Japanese naval radio traffic, traffic it could not read except for ship call signs. On December 2, the call signs for most of Japan's aircraft carriers disappeared from the airwaves — just as they had before the Japanese invaded Indochina. But where were the carriers heading? When Lieutenant Commander Edwin Layton, Admiral Kimmel's intelligence officer, informed him of this disquieting fact, the admiral is reputed to have replied, "Do you mean to say they could be rounding Diamond Head and you wouldn't know it?"

official. He arrived on a Japanese liner in March 1941 and set out to amass information on a huge scale. He was driven around the island by a consular chauffeur and found it easy to spy on the Army and Navy bases, to identify the ships in harbor, and to record their movements and habits — including the low level of activity in the fleet on weekends. He also suborned civilian staff of Japanese extraction who were working at bases and living quarters in many humble capacities such as drivers, gardeners, and servants — all ideally placed to garner information on personnel and facilities.

Yoshikawa's invaluable harvest was supplemented in the last days of peace by three professional spies of the Japanese Navy's Third Bureau (intelligence), who made secret visits to Oahu. One was a submariner, one a midget-submarine specialist, and the third, Lieutenant Commander Suguru Suzuki, was an airman and close colleague of Genda's. These officers took advantage of a special agreement between Washington and Tokyo allowing three Japanese merchant ships to sail through sanctions and visit American Pacific ports, including Honolulu, in October and November of 1941. Suzuki, the most important member of the trio, was privy to the Pearl Harbor plan and knew exactly what information was needed. He sailed on the last of the three ships, the *Taiyo Maru*, ostensibly as assistant purser. The vessel broadly followed the northerly transpacific route chosen for the attacking force, enabling Suzuki to note weather conditions and the likelihood of being spotted by planes or ships. No ship was sighted, but a US reconnaissance aircraft was seen 200 miles north of Oahu, at which point it turned back. Later, US combat planes made mock-attack passes over the ship before returning to base. Suzuki therefore advised the task force commander to launch his attack from farther than 200 miles north.

The Japanese consul general in Honolulu, Nagao Kita, boarded the vessel several times at Honolulu on November 1 and 2, to brief Suzuki (Yoshikawa stayed away for security reasons). Kita was able to smuggle sensitive documents crammed with information inside newspapers he openly took aboard under the noses of American security guards at the gangways. Suzuki scanned the coastline and the port area and noted the low level of activity and security on November 2, a Sunday. The spy dared not leave the ship but could just make out Pearl Harbor, about eight miles away, from the bridge with his high-powered naval binoculars. Suzuki gave Kita a questionnaire with over one hundred queries for Yoshikawa to answer overnight as best he could and return via the consul. Thus on his return to Japan, Suzuki was able to provide the naval staff preparing the attack, including Genda, with invaluable fresh material at special briefings.

A few months before that, the consulate, which had been feeding information to Tokyo for use in planning the attack, was ordered to superimpose a grid of numbered squares on a map of Pearl Harbor in order to clarify its frequent reports on which American warships were where. This crucial message was intercepted by American intelligence but was not forwarded to those who most needed to know — the commands on Oahu, who might have responded with appropriate alarm. On December 3, as the attack force approached the halfway mark, a long message from the consulate, sent to Tokyo for forwarding to the Navy and listing warships in harbor with their positions, was also intercepted. But because of the sheer weight of signal traffic and the low priority given to RED MAGIC, it was not deciphered until December 11 — four days after the attack.

THE ROOSEVELT ADMINISTRATION, FOCUSED ON THE WAR IN EUROPE AND ANXIOUS NOT TO provoke war with Japan — at least not before its forces were ready (March 1942 was the Army's earliest estimate) — pursued the diplomatic route to the bitter end. US policy was that in the likely event of war, Japan *must* be seen to strike the first blow — the only way to silence the isolationists. Talks dragged on in Washington between Secretary of State Cordell Hull and his staff, and Kichisaburo Nomura, the well-liked ex-admiral and ambassador to Washington, supported in the last stages by Special Envoy Saburo Kurusu.

The pair called on Hull on November 18 but that round of talks broke down over Japanese adherence to the Axis. Two days later, they were back with Tokyo's final proposal for an accommodation, which Nomura for one knew the Americans would never accept. The demands included an end to sanctions and to US aid to China in exchange for a vague commitment to withdraw Japanese forces from Indochina. Hull responded on November 26 with an American proposal requiring Japan to halt its expansion, to reduce its presence in Indochina, and to negotiate with the Chinese Nationalists led by Chiang Kai-shek, in exchange for a limited lifting of sanctions. Nobody on the American side believed Tokyo would accept the loss of face involved in such a retreat and the talks duly broke down.

The administration's known policy of leaving the first shot to Japan appeased the isolationists but handed the choice on whether, when, and how war would begin to Japan, with its well-established tradition of starting wars with surprise attacks. Also on November 26, British intelligence reached the Americans of a southbound Japanese convoy with 50,000 troops, already south of Formosa. Hull therefore called a second meeting with the two envoys to demand an immediate withdrawal from Indochina and China. The amazed diplomats abandoned their habitual politeness and told Hull unequivocally that there was no point in forwarding such a demand to Tokyo. But they did. The standoff now appeared to be cast in stone.

The Emperor's Spies

In preparation for a possible surprise attack, Japanese spies created detailed reports of the American strength at Pearl Harbor, noting all ship movements. (Below) This map of the entrance to Pearl Harbor was sketched by secret agent Suguru Suzuki when photographs and other material he had gathered on a trip to Hawaii were mislaid. (Bottom) While plans for the attack proceeded, Japan's popular ambassador to the United Sates, the retired admiral, Kichisaburo Nomura (center, in photo) kept diplomatic channels open.

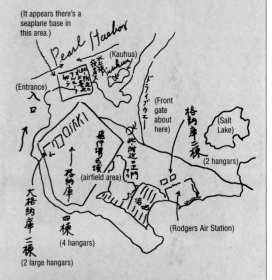

On the Town in Honolulu

"This bloody awful hole" is how one sailor described Pearl Harbor in the months before the war. For the thousands of Navy enlisted men and recently called up reservists on the warships of the Pacific Fleet, Hawaii was anything but a vacation spot. In port, they spent most of their days in mindless and repetitive maintenance work, and most of their nights crammed into spartan and sweltering quarters deep belowdecks. Their only real break was the occasional shore liberty.

All the taxis and buses from Merry Point Landing in Pearl Harbor unloaded their passengers at the Army-Navy YMCA on Hotel Street. Many men bought a first drink at the Black Cat Café across the street, later immortalized in James Jones' *From Here to Eternity*. Then, along with hundreds of other soldiers and sailors, they worked their way down Hotel Street — a narrow thoroughfare lined with rickety wooden buildings, choked with people and traffic, and perfumed with "the unique smell of Honolulu," to quote Theodore Mason, author of *Battleship Sailor*, "a malodorous infusion of decaying pork, overripe fish, and a variety of pungent spices unknown to Western nostrils." Depending on their mood, the men paused in bars that caught their fancy or to have their pictures taken or to buy a tacky souvenir (like the one at left, probably made in Japan). Some eventually ventured onto one of the even seedier sidestreets of the red-light district.

Here, as throughout Honolulu, the enlisted sailor was the lowest of the low in the social pecking order. The shore-based Army boys — reliable customers who visited regularly — always came first. But if you hadn't lost most of your money at poker back on the ship or buying drinks and trinkets on Hotel Street, you might just be able to get yourself ten minutes with a girl from stateside — three dollars was the going rate — imported and sanctioned (unofficially) by the military, in rooms or clubs that were subject to regular health inspection. For most, however, the boat ride back to the ship transpired in drunken, sullen disappointment.

Nonetheless, as Mason remembers it, there was something wonderful about those prewar days in Hawaii, a mood of "boisterous innocence" that would disappear forever on December 7, 1941.

(Above) Raymond Brittain, left, of the USS *Tennessee* and two shipmates on leave in Honolulu on December 6, 1941. (Below) An obviously posed magazine shot shows clean-cut servicemen joining in Flag Day celebrations, May 1941.

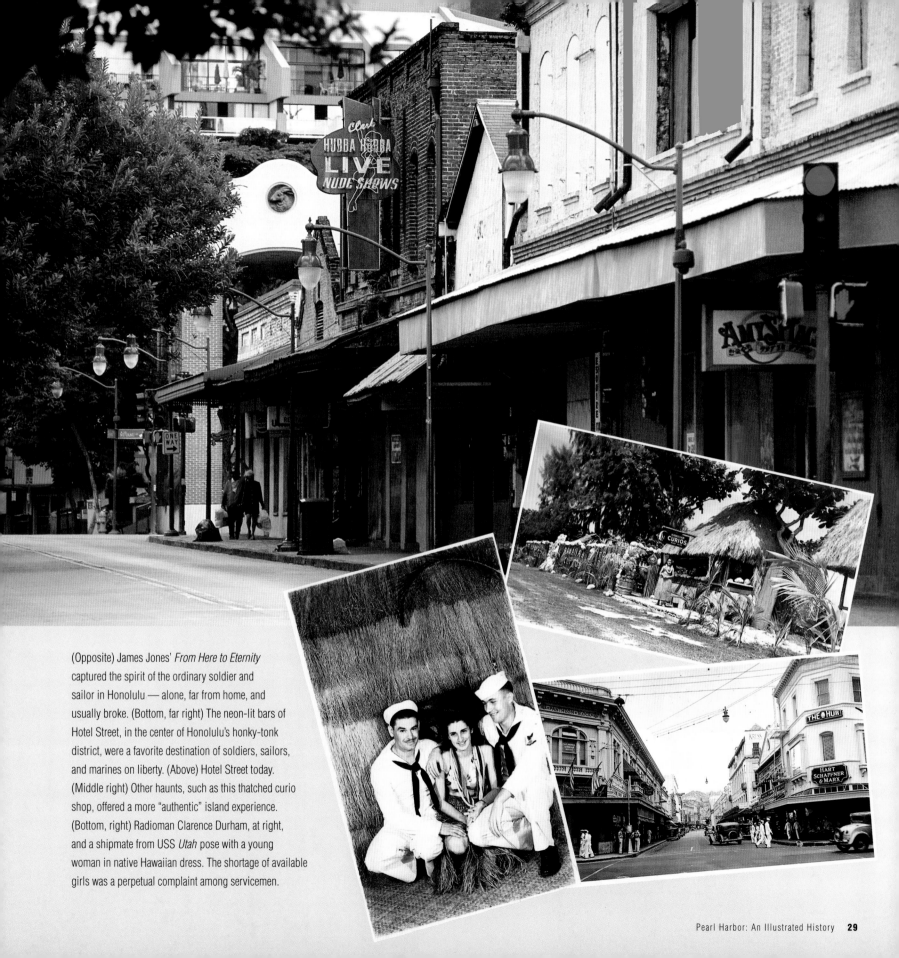

(Opposite) James Jones' *From Here to Eternity* captured the spirit of the ordinary soldier and sailor in Honolulu — alone, far from home, and usually broke. (Bottom, far right) The neon-lit bars of Hotel Street, in the center of Honolulu's honky-tonk district, were a favorite destination of soldiers, sailors, and marines on liberty. (Above) Hotel Street today. (Middle right) Other haunts, such as this thatched curio shop, offered a more "authentic" island experience. (Bottom, right) Radioman Clarence Durham, at right, and a shipmate from USS *Utah* pose with a young woman in native Hawaiian dress. The shortage of available girls was a perpetual complaint among servicemen.

Officers and Gentlemen

In *Faith of My Fathers*, John McCain describes the life of his father, John McCain II (later, a full admiral), on being posted to Pearl Harbor as a young submarine officer in 1934. "Hawaii in the 1930s was the heart of Navy culture, where singular standards of social etiquette and personal and professional ethics were rarely breached. . . .Newly arrived officers, dressed in white uniforms, took their wives, who were attired in white gloves and hats, to call on the families of fellow officers every Wednesday and Saturday between four and six o'clock." On Saturdays, McCain's parents would attend the four o'clock tea dance at the Royal Hawaiian Hotel before returning home to dress for a formal dinner-dance at the Pearl Harbor Submarine Club. Even when they dined at home in their tiny officer's bungalow, McCain's father wore black tie and his mother a long gown.

(Above) Lieutenant General Walter C. Short, left, and Admiral Husband E. Kimmel flank the man who perhaps personified the "officer as gentleman," Lord Louis Mountbatten. A British naval commander and cousin of King George VI, Mountbatten visited Hawaii in early fall 1941 during a brief tour of the United States. (Left) The art deco façade of Lockwood Hall at Pearl Harbor's submarine base. In 1941, this building housed Admiral Kimmel's CINCPAC headquarters. (Opposite) The Royal Hawaiian Hotel today, and (inset) as it appeared prewar, when it hosted the Saturday tea dances frequented by officers and their wives. (Top) For Sunday morning, December 7, 1941, Kimmel and Short had scheduled their regular round of golf.

This genteel society existed at some remove from the bars and tattoo joints of Hotel Street frequented by enlisted men, and the gulf was intentional. The professional distinctions between officers and their men — needed to maintain order and discipline — were reinforced by social distance. The manners of polite society also supported the code of honor to which an officer and a gentleman was — and still is — expected to adhere. In addition to the well-known admonitions not to "lie, cheat, or steal" are the more solemn obligations that an officer not risk his men's lives unnecessarily nor cause them to suffer a penalty that only he deserves.

The two commanders at the apex of military culture on Oahu had advanced their careers by hewing closely to military tradition. Admiral Husband E. Kimmel, Commander in Chief of the Pacific Fleet (CINCPAC), even disapproved of the Navy's new khakis as "lessening the dignity of the wearer." For relaxation, he preferred a brisk walk with some of his officers to more convivial gatherings at which he was often stiff and uncomfortable.

His opposite number, Lieutenant General Walter C. Short, was slightly more at ease with the social obligations that went with the job. On the Saturday evening before the attack, Short and his wife were guests at the Schofield Barracks Officers' Club for a gala featuring a benefit show of amateur singing and dancing. But by 9:30, the Shorts were on their way home. As their staff car headed toward town, Pearl Harbor and its ships lay lit up before them. "Isn't that a beautiful sight?" commented the general. Then he paused, adding, "and what a target they would make."

Schofield Barracks

Once called "the most beautiful barracks in the world" by novelist James Jones, Schofield Barracks on Oahu also laid claim to being the US Army's largest housing unit in 1941. Its 1930s buildings (opposite, top) are laid out around huge quadrangles, entered through impressive gates (below) that have weathered over the years (left). (Opposite left, top) In mid-November 1940, the Army honored the Navy with a review at Schofield attended by Admiral Kimmel, in dress whites. In 1952, the barracks served as a backdrop for the filming of *From Here to Eternity* (opposite, right), which later played at Schofield's own movie theater (opposite left, bottom).

Hickam Field

Home to the Army's Hawaiian Air Force (HAF), Hickam Field was constructed as part of the buildup of military installations on Oahu during the 1930s. Its sweeping art deco gates (above) still welcome visitors to the base (right). Although now a modern air base (bottom), Hickam's period architecture has been preserved in its original water tower (below, left) and in the Fifteenth Air Base Wing headquarters (below, right).

CHAPTER TWO

On the Brink

"Do you mean to say they could be rounding Diamond Head and you wouldn't know it?"

— Admiral Kimmel on December 2, 1941,
after being told by his intelligence officer that the radio call
signs for Japanese carriers had disappeared.

This dispatch is to be considered a war warning. Negotiations with Japan have ceased and an aggressive move by Japan is expected within the next few days. Japanese troops and naval task forces indicate an amphibious expedition against either the Philippines, Thai or Kra Peninsula or possibly Borneo. Execute an appropriate defensive deployment.

THE CHOICE OF THE GRAPHIC PHRASE "WAR WARNING" IN CHIEF OF NAVAL OPERATIONS Admiral Harold R. Stark's November 27 note to Admiral Kimmel set the message apart from previous alerts from the Navy Department to its great fortress in the Pacific. Washington now viewed US-Japanese relations as desperate. Equally clear from the wordy message is that Washington did not specifically expect an attack on Pearl Harbor. Indeed, there was no sign of one, whereas there was every indication of an imminent southward attack from French Indochina. But Washington did not bother to forward to Pearl Harbor several interceptions of Japanese radio traffic that, especially with hindsight, could be seen as harbingers of a raid on Hawaii.

Acting by the Book: The Pearl Harbor Commanders

One quality shared by the two top officers of the Army and Navy on Oahu was a firm belief in following military procedure to the letter. Admiral Husband E. Kimmel, born at Henderson, Kentucky, in 1882, graduated from the US Naval Academy at Annapolis, Maryland, in 1904 and pursued a glittering career as an accomplished and versatile officer, rising to command a battleship in 1933. In 1934, he became chief of staff to the Commander, Battleships, US Fleet. By 1939, he was a rear admiral and Commander, Cruisers, Battle Force. He was known as a stickler for rules and discipline. With his heavy features and lack of small talk, Kimmel gave a sturdily humorless impression; his unimpeachable record showed no trace of imagination or inspiration. But he had energy and an eye for able subordinates, giving and receiving unstinted loyalty despite a hot temper on a short fuse.

On Kimmel's elevation in January 1941, over the heads of a raft of senior candidates, he jumped two ranks to become admiral. Kimmel's substantive post was Commander in Chief, Pacific Fleet (CINCPAC), comprising three-quarters of the US Navy.

(Above) Admiral Husband E. Kimmel. (Below) Lieutenant General Walter C. Short.

Lieutenant General Walter C. Short, born in Fillmore, Illinois, was two years older than his naval colleague and was directly commissioned into the infantry on graduation from university in 1902, at the age of twenty-two. He was among the first US servicemen to sail for France in 1917. A training specialist rather than a fighting leader, he stayed with the Third Army in Germany until July 1919. Only in 1920 was he promoted to major and sent to Staff School; he was awarded his first general's star in 1937. He gained his third on being posted to Hawaii, at the same time as Kimmel received his promotion.

Unlike the strongly built admiral, with whom he quickly struck up a close rapport, Short did not look the part. A lean man with gaunt features and striking eyes, he might have been a professor except for the uniform. Indeed, his main professional interest was training, which dominated his thinking even as a commander of major fighting units. Invincibly reserved and always courteous, Short was not overendowed with originality, but nobody questioned his competence or diligence. He and Kimmel took to playing golf on alternate Sunday mornings; they were due to tee off as usual on December 7, 1941.

(Pages 36–37) An aerial shot of Hickam Field, with Diamond Head in the distance.

Short received a similar message that same day, from General George C. Marshall, chief of staff of the United States Army. Be wary, Marshall told him, and "take such reconnaissance and other measures as you deem necessary but not to alarm civil population." The warnings from Washington were prompted by a breakdown in negotiations with Japan on the previous day, November 26. Secretary of State Hull and the two Japanese envoys, Nomura and Kurusu, were so far from an understanding that President Roosevelt was considering a summit meeting with Emperor Hirohito to break the deadlock in the struggle to achieve a "modus vivendi" with the aggressive Japanese, known to be on the verge of breaking out southward.

The news from Japan had been getting worse and worse for a decade, as Kimmel and Short well knew. They also knew that a surprise attack was the favorite Japanese military opening gambit, and that the US fleet was the only force capable of confronting Japan on anything like equal terms. The Hawaiian commanders' duty was not to worry about what might happen in Borneo or the Philippines but only to look after the US battlefleet and its base. Their job was to be prepared for the worst case — a Japanese attack at any time, however it might come, whether over, on, or under the sea or possibly all three. The commanders and their staffs had discussed this many times — among themselves, with each other, with their superiors, and with the administration in Washington. The admiral and the general knew in their *minds* that Pearl Harbor must be high on the Japanese agenda of aggression — but the evidence suggests that in their *hearts* they did not believe it would happen.

Kimmel fortunately stepped up precautions, against submarine attack at least, with increased destroyer patrols, but did not order extra aerial reconnaissance around Oahu. He did not have enough aircraft for a 360-degree, around-the-clock watch but behaved as though the inability to cover every angle at all times was an excuse to cover none. He did not try to make the best of what he had, clearly discounting the possibility of air attack. Short assumed the Navy was taking care of reconnaissance and took no action on it. Instead, he prepared for sabotage by ethnic Japanese and/or spies, disarming and tightly grouping his aircraft while locking away munitions to make life harder for the phantom terrorists. Each commander was determined not to allow training routines to be interrupted by alarms and excursions elsewhere. There had been alerts before, leading nowhere. The usual generous local weekend leave was allowed from the evening of Friday, December 5.

The defenders of Oahu could hardly have been less prepared psychologically. It could be argued that Kimmel and Short should have been ordered expressly to prepare for an early attack on Hawaii. On the other hand, Washington was surely entitled to expect commanders of such seniority to do what was necessary without a reminder in every new crisis.

On orders from Lieutenant General Walter C. Short, B-18 Bolo bombers (below) at Hickam Field are parked wingtip to wingtip, to protect them against possible attacks by saboteurs. Unfortunately, this made them easy targets for the Japanese bombers.

"*The moment has arrived. The rise or fall of our empire is at stake. . . .*"

— from Admiral Yamamoto's final radio message to the striking force

THE CLANKING OF HEAVY WINDLASSES ECHOED ACROSS HITOKAPPU BAY ON A BLEAK AND cold morning at Etorofu in the Kurile Islands. An anxious Vice Admiral Chuichi Nagumo had ordered his twenty-three warships and their eight oil tankers to raise anchors. The date: November 26, 1941. Destination: Hawaii. Yamamoto himself had chosen the approach, eastward and then south-eastward across the inhospitable and usually empty waters of the northern Pacific, then due south for the last few hours of the approach to the selected launching point, set on Suzuki's advice at 230 miles north of Oahu.

Nagumo had announced the objective of the task force on November 23, once all its disparate units had assembled in Hitokappu Bay. A conference of captains and commanders aboard the force flagship *Akagi* was first stunned, then elated as Nagumo's chief of staff, Rear Admiral Ryunosuke Kusaka, took over the briefing, calling on a succession of specialists to expound the various aspects of a complicated plan. Both admirals were convinced that a single attack in two waves would be enough. They saw no point in a much more risky follow-up attack, although they paid lip service to it to mollify the airmen, especially Genda and Commander Mitsuo Fuchida, overall leader of the striking force's planes.

The pair led a second conference for flight commanders in the afternoon to lay out the plan of attack. One hour before the first wave struck, two reconnaissance seaplanes from the cruisers escorting the carriers would be sent southward. One

(Opposite) The flight deck of the *Akagi*, flagship of the Japanese force, in Hitokappu Bay. Maintenance crews work on the planes parked on the ship's flight deck. (Above) To protect against damage from bomb and shell splinters, rolled-up matresses are strapped to *Akagi*'s bridge.

would check Pearl Harbor; the other, the alternative US fleet anchorage at Lahaina, a deep-water bay on the western side of the island of Maui, about halfway between Oahu and the "Big Island" of Hawaii to the southeast. (The Japanese would have been delighted to find the fleet at Lahaina because any ship sunk there would stay sunk, in many hundreds of feet of water. But the US Navy had all but given up using it.) Each wave would assemble in turn over the carriers in time to start bombing Oahu at 7:30 A.M. local time (in 1941, equivalent to 6 P.M. GMT, 1 P.M. in Washington, and 4 A.M. the next day in Japan; nowadays, Hawaii is ten full hours behind GMT all year round).

According to plan, each Japanese carrier would keep back nine interceptors to protect the ships while the attackers were away. One of three groups of eighteen apiece would be in the air at all times as a combat air patrol. The first wave of the attack would comprise 189 planes. Fifty horizontal or high-level Nakajima B5N2 (known to the Americans as "Kate") bombers would be led by Fuchida himself. Forty Kates in their other, interchangeable role

as torpedo bombers would fly under Lieutenant Shigeharu Murata, while fifty-four Aichi D3A1 "Val" dive-bombers would be led by Lieutenant Commander Kakuichi Takahashi. And forty-five Mitsubishi A6M2 fighters, the formidable Zeros, headed by Lieutenant Commander Shigeru Itaya, were to seize and hold the airspace over Oahu and to strafe ships and ground targets.

The torpedo bombers would attack first, descending to a level as low as thirty feet, well below the height of a battleship's masthead, and concentrating on the largest ships. The Japanese knew the American battleships were moored in pairs. The torpedo bombers would hit the outside ships. They would be followed by the horizontals to take out any battleships the torpedo bombers couldn't. Then the dive-bombers would go in, hitting the Army airfields at Hickam and Wheeler, the main Navy one on Ford Island, and the seaplane base at Kaneohe Bay. This would forestall pursuit by the defenders and cause maximum damage.

The second wave would strike an hour after the first. Under the overall command of Lieutenant Commander Shigekazu Shimazaki, leading fifty-four high-level Kates, it would also include eighty-one Vals under Lieutenant Commander Takashige Egusa and thirty-six Zeros under Lieutenant Saburo Shindo, for a total of 171 aircraft. No stage-two Kates carried torpedoes. These weapons were best unleashed by aircraft with a clear view, approaching slowly and steadily at low level. Only the surprise effect of the first wave could offset their resulting vulnerability. The second

Commander Mitsuo Fuchida (above) would serve as overall leader of the striking force's planes once they were in the air. (Opposite) *Kaga* and *Zuikaku* steam astern of *Akagi* on the way to Hawaii.

wave would bomb and strafe Hickam and Ford Island again, as well as the naval air station at Kaneohe and the Army's Wheeler. The dive-bombers would complete the destruction begun by the first wave's torpedoes. All pilots agreed to preserve radio silence before the attack began, even if shot down or forced to ditch in the sea.

After leading the first wave, Fuchida planned to stay on over Oahu. He was determined to leave the scene last after carefully observing and recording the damage inflicted. As a veteran, he knew that all combat fliers tended to exaggerate the impact of their attacks — a near-miss could produce a spectacular effect without doing much harm to the target.

Admiral Chuichi Nagumo, Commander of the Carrier Force

He was an unlikely choice to lead the most daring and difficult mission of the entire Japanese southward advance. Chuichi Nagumo, with no experience in maritime aviation, was put in charge of an air strike intended to achieve strategic surprise across thousands of miles of land and sea. Born in Honshu in 1887, Nagumo distinguished himself at the naval academy at Eta Jima prior to a series of seaborne posts interrupted by tours of duty in the West. Although he discharged various staff jobs well enough, he came into his own at sea. He successively commanded a light cruiser, a destroyer division and, in 1934, a battleship. A year later, he made the big career jump to rear admiral, serving in China as commander of a cruiser division. In 1939, he took over a squadron of battleships and was promoted to vice admiral. Command of the elite First Air Fleet came his way by seniority, but Nagumo had a very capable and strong-minded chief of staff, Rear Admiral Ryunosuke Kusaka, who had lengthy experience with carriers. With his sturdy figure and swaggering, gladhanding manner, Nagumo was unusual in the degree of concern he showed for his men. But there was an underlying anxiety within him that became ever more apparent with advancing age and responsibility.

The Japanese knew from their indefatigable consulate that there were no antiaircraft barrage balloons over Oahu and no torpedo nets protecting individual ships. But they had no means of knowing whether the torpedo nets across the mouth of the only channel serving the harbor would be closed or open. If open, all well and good; if not, torpedoes and quite possibly planes would have to be sacrificed to blast an opening.

Such was the scheme, as intricate as any battle plan ever drawn up, for knocking the United States battlefleet out of the coming war for at least six months. Every eventuality seemed to have been accounted for in a design fifteen times more complicated than its model, the British raid on Taranto — except, inevitably, for several eventualities that arose on the day. The pilots made their plans with the aid of a three-dimensional detailed model of Pearl Harbor aboard *Akagi,* until they knew it by heart and it came to them in their dreams. The model was constantly adjusted to take account of every scrap of new information from Honolulu, even after the powerful task force — along with its eight oil tankers — had slipped out of their Kurile Islands anchorage. And the briefings of aircrews continued, even though Genda's vocal cords all but gave out after the first two days.

✪

THE JAPANESE DEPLOYMENT AGAINST THE UNITED STATES FLEET was the largest and most powerful assemblage of seapower so far gathered in the Pacific Ocean.

Admiral Nagumo's Mobile Force had recently swelled by two new fleet carriers. The Fifth Carrier Division (*Shokaku, Zuikaku*) joined the First (*Akagi, Kaga*) and Second (*Hiryu, Soryu*) of the First Air Fleet, giving the commander a total of more than four hundred planes. The carriers were screened by three submarines and a light cruiser leading nine destroyers; big-gun protection was provided by two battleships and two heavy cruisers. A Special Submarine Attack Unit of twenty-seven boats was deployed separately and directly from Japan. Five of them carried battery-powered, midget submarines on their decks, piggyback fashion, to be launched against Pearl Harbor from close range. Nagumo, a cautious man who grew ever more anxious with advancing age and responsibility, did not like this embellishment — rightly fearing that the submarines could give the game away before his aircraft struck.

THE BEST EFFORTS OF REVISIONIST HISTO-rians, convinced that President Roosevelt colluded with the attack to force American entry into the war, have never proved that Nagumo's fleet emitted a single signal that might have betrayed its approach. The orders for Operation "Z" (named after the code flag flown by Admiral Togo ordering the attack at Tsushima) had been delivered by hand and/or by teleprinter connected to land lines. Nagumo's fleet sailed in strict radio silence. Ship-to-ship communication was via flags or signal lamp. Planes and ship radios had been disabled. While the vessels plowed quietly on, back home the Japanese mounted a ruse to fool any eaves-droppers. Because skilled listeners can recognize an individual's distinct tapping style on a Morse key, the regular operators from Nagumo's ships were deliberately left behind. They kept up a barrage of messages, giving the impression that the attacking armada was still very much in Japanese home waters. While the attacking force dared not transmit, there was of course no risk in receiving messages. After all, it might be necessary to call off the attack if the United States accepted Japan's demands. Telegraphists remained on maximum alert around the clock.

Yamamoto sent Nagumo a brief coded message at 5:30 P.M. on December 2: "Climb Mount Niitaka 1208." The refer-ence was to the Empire's tallest peak, located in Formosa — a fitting code phrase for a mission of such grand scale. Nagumo knew what this meant. The diplo-matic option was exhausted and hostilities would be opened, by the customary pre-emptive strike, against the United States on December 8, Tokyo time.

(Above) An officer aboard *Kaga* briefs pilots on the attack using a chalk sketch of Pearl Harbor. (Right) The fleet, from a vantage point aboard *Akagi*. (Below) To avoid detection, the Japanese fleet sailed far to the north into what was called the "empty sea," before swinging south to attack Hawaii.

(Pages 46–47) Artist Tom Freeman's dramatic depiction of the Japanese carrier force advancing toward Pearl Harbor.

November 26, 1941

NAGUMO'S STRIKING FORCE

December 7, 1941

CHAPTER THREE

First Shot, Last Warning

*"Negotiations with the Japanese appear to be terminated. . . .
Japanese future action unpredictable but hostile action possible at any moment."*

— From a telegram sent to Army and Navy commanders in the Philippines,
the Panama Canal, and Hawaii on November 27, 1941

THE MAP OF THE ISLAND OF OAHU ROUGHLY RESEMBLES A BROAD-BLADED MEAT CLEAVER, with the socket for the absent handle below and to the right (at the southeast). In the middle of the lower edge of the blade is a deep indentation shaped like a cloverleaf on a stalk — Pearl Harbor. The stalk is the entrance channel; the spread of leaves to the north of it are the "lochs" — West, Middle, East, and Southeast. Between the two last-named areas of seawater lies Ford Island, an oblong aligned from northeast to southwest and topped with an airfield complete with tower and hangars, administrative buildings, and living quarters. In 1941, the battleships always moored alongside the long southeastern shore of Ford Island, usually in pairs, with their bows pointing toward the channel to the southwest.

On December 7, seven were tied up there; an eighth, USS *Pennsylvania*, fleet flagship, was in dry dock to the south of Ford. The northernmost afloat was *Nevada*, alone; then *Arizona*, with the repair ship *Vestal* outside to port; *Tennessee* (inboard) and *West Virginia*; *Maryland* and *Oklahoma* (outboard); tanker *Neosho*, alone; *California*, flag of the battleship force, alone; and finally, seaplane tender *Avocet*, alone. The long northwest side of Ford was reserved for the aircraft carriers, but as there were just three in the Pacific Fleet, none of which was in port this day, other ships tied up there, too. There were two light cruisers (*Detroit*, *Raleigh*), an old battleship (*Utah*) turned training and target ship, and a seaplane tender (*Tangier*). In all, some 185 United States Navy ships of all shapes and sizes — about half the Pacific Fleet in number — were in harbor that Sunday.

(1) USS *Detroit*
(2) USS *Raleigh*
(3) USS *Utah*
(4) USS *Tangier*
(5) USS *Nevada*
(6) USS *Arizona*
(7) USS *Vestal*
(8) USS *Tennessee*
(9) USS *West Virginia*
(10) USS *Maryland*
(11) USS *Oklahoma*
(12) USS *Neosho*
(13) USS *California*
(14) USS *Pennsylvania*
(15) USS *Oglala*
(16) USS *Helena*
(17) USS *Shaw*
(18) USS *Avocet*

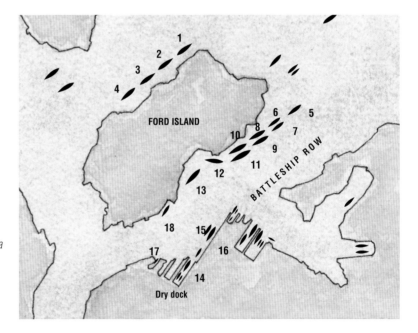

(Pages 48–49) A contemporary photograph of Ford Island at dawn. (Opposite) Concrete moorings in the waters along the southeast shore of Ford Island (top) still bear the names of the battleships tied there on the morning of December 7, 1941. These two honor the *West Virginia* (lower left) and *Tennessee* (lower right).

Battleship *Colorado* and carrier *Saratoga* were lucky enough to be on the American west coast. USS *Enterprise* was on her way back from reinforcing Wake Island, far to the west, with a Marine Corps fighter squadron. And *Lexington* was bound for Midway, also well to the west, on a similar errand. A total of twelve cruisers, thirty-six destroyers, and eighteen submarines were out of port on various routine missions, including the carriers' strong escorts. In tonnage terms, considerably more than half the US Navy, including the bulk of its battleship force, was in harbor.

On the "mainland" shore to the south, across the water from Ford Island, stood (from west to east) the naval hospital, the headquarters of the Fourteenth Naval District commanded by Rear Admiral Claude C. Bloch, a signal tower, and a large navy yard with docks, dry docks, and other repair facilities. East from the yard is a spit of land called Kuahua which then carried a railhead, and south of that, across an inlet, is a small promontory, site of the submarine base and headquarters of the Commander in Chief, Pacific Fleet (CINCPAC). Inland from there immediately to the east was one of two tank farms holding fuel for the fleet (the other lay south of the naval hospital, over to the west). The Army's Hawaiian Air Force ran Hickam Field, due south of Ford Island and the Navy Yard. To the west of the 12,600-acre harbor complex lay the small Marine Corps air station at Ewa near Barbers Point.

(Opposite) An aerial view of Pearl Harbor as it looked in 1941. Early on the morning of December 7, the Japanese first wave would have a similar view as its attacking planes swooped down on unsuspecting Ford Island, Hickam and Wheeler Fields, and Battleship Row. (Above) This tower still stands near CINCPAC headquarters.

AT 0342 ON THE MORNING OF DECEMBER 7, Ensign R.C. McCloy, the duty officer on the bridge of the minesweeper *Condor*, sighted a periscope some fifty yards ahead and to port. *Condor* was one of the vessels patrolling the security zone off the entrance to Pearl Harbor. After watching through his binoculars for a few minutes, Quartermaster Second Class R.C. Uttrick confirmed the sighting. The two men reported it at 0357 by signal lamp to the faster and more heavily armed destroyer *Ward*, also on patrol outside the harbor. The *Ward* had acquired a new captain only two days before, Lieutenant William W. Outerbridge, thirty-five years old. The destroyer was his first command, and its assignment that night — his first at sea as skipper — was to cover a three-mile square immediately off the harbor entrance. Standing orders stated that any

Ford Island

Battleship Row

Tank farm

● CINCPAC Headquarters

Hickam Field

Tank farm

Entrance to Pearl Harbor

At 0342 on December 7, 1941, the minesweeper *Condor* (below right) spotted what looked like a periscope just outside the entrance to Pearl Harbor (above, as it looks today.) The minesweeper signaled the patrolling destroyer *Ward* (below left), which searched the waters for half an hour but found nothing. Despite the alarm, the gate to the torpedo net across the harbor entrance was opened at 0448 to admit the *Condor* — and then left open, as other ships were expected to arrive shortly.

unreported submarine in the restricted area around the entrance was to be attacked and sunk. Outerbridge ordered all his crew to General Quarters (action stations) and conducted a sonar search, but found nothing. The sighting was therefore discounted and not reported to District or CINCPAC headquarters. At 0435, Outerbridge resumed patrol. Thirteen minutes later, the boom and net "gate" across the entrance to Pearl Harbor was opened to admit the *Condor* and her sister, USS *Crossbill*. As more ships were expected to pass in and out in the ensuing hours, the torpedo barrier was left open.

THE JAPANESE AVIATORS, LED BY GENDA AND FUCHIDA, HAD BEEN TOTALLY OPPOSED TO Yamamoto's inclusion of an independent attack by submarines from Japan to back up the air strike in case that high-risk enterprise proved inadequate. The subs could easily give the game away, the airmen reasoned. The boats' duties included reconnaissance and lying in wait in Hawaiian waters for US vessels either on their way to Pearl Harbor or coming out to hunt the attackers. Five of the largest carried one short-range midget submarine each, clamped to their decks, for launching as close as possible to Pearl Harbor.

The "mother boats" approached Oahu on the surface under cover of darkness. At about midnight on the night of December 6 to 7, the two-man crews boarded the midgets. The battery-powered boats were 78 feet long and displaced just 46 tons, but were capable of a remarkable 23 knots surfaced (in calm conditions) and 19 submerged, albeit for short bursts only — once their batteries were exhausted, they were dead in the water. Even at moderate speeds, they had a range of only 80 miles surfaced or 18 underwater. The mother ships submerged and worked up to their maximum underwater speed of 8 knots to give their offspring the fastest possible start.

Their assignment was to penetrate the harbor, lie in wait on the bottom until the air attack started, launch their two torpedoes amid the inevitable pandemonium, and then steal away. The trick was to get into the harbor in the first place, a maneuver best executed in the wake of incoming ships such as the *Condor* or the *Crossbill*. The midget sub on *I-24*, commanded by Ensign Kazuo Sakamaki, had a defective gyrocompass but the keen young officer decided to go ahead anyway — even though the defect made steering a steady course virtually impossible.

THE *WARD* WAS STILL ON PATROL WHEN USS *ANTARES*, A STORES SHIP TOWING A LIGHTER, arrived off the entrance to Pearl Harbor to await a tug. The ship's lookouts raised the alarm at 0630 after sighting the conning tower of a small submarine three-quarters of a mile ahead and to starboard. Outerbridge, summoned from his bunk, saw that the submarine was now brazenly following in the wake of *Antares* as she set off into the channel. Once again, he ordered General Quarters. The old destroyer dashed ahead and opened fire at seventy-five yards, the guns depressed as far as they would go. The first round overshot but the second struck at the waterline, at the junction of the hull and the conning tower. For good measure, the *Ward* dropped a pattern of four depth charges over the stern as she swept on past, narrowly missing the *Antares*. The submarine sank in twelve hundred feet of water.

Thus it was that the first shot of the war in the Pacific was fired by the United States — an American destroyer bombarding a Japanese submarine, the first vessel lost in what was to become the largest and most destructive naval campaign in history. Outerbridge sent a signal at 0653 to the District Command: "We have attacked, fired upon, and dropped depth charges upon submarine operating in defensive sea area." Minutes later, a PBY patrol aircraft from Ford Island reported depth-charging a submarine one mile off the harbor entrance.

The various reports of submarine sightings were the subject of long and inconclusive debate in a welter of telephone calls among staff officers ashore, often at cross-purposes. Admiral Kimmel was not told until well after 0700. Worse, the Navy did not bother to inform the Army, which might conceivably have raised its vigilance from a low-level alert against sabotage — mounting a radar watch, manning the coastal and antiaircraft guns, dispersing its planes, and adding extra aerial reconnaissance, as well as putting fighters on standby.

⭐

ON THE CARRIERS PITCHING INTO THE wind at more than twenty knots in the chill waters of the "empty sea," tension had risen as the barometer sank. Japanese ships kept Tokyo time wherever they were. According to the chronometers, it was approaching 0200 on December 8, but where they were, the sailors of the Mobile Force had yet to see the dawn of the 7th. Aboard flagship *Akagi,* on the heaving, wood-lined deck in the shelter of the "island" superstructure, the airmen stood at attention opposite Admiral Nagumo and his staff. The two groups of men, shifting their weight to keep their balance, toasted each other with small glasses of sake and bowed stiffly. No matter what the consequences might be, everyone knew that the fate of nations, especially their own, hung on what was about to start. Many pilots wore samurai scarves wrapped around their aviator helmets. Fuchida's maintenance crew presented the deeply moved commander with a headband especially made for the unique occasion. Fuchida had added a couple of his own sartorial details to his uniform that morning — a red shirt and underwear that would mask from his crew any wounds he might receive.

Admiral Togo's original flag, soiled and tattered from the Battle of Tsushima, was broken out on the signal mast — initiating the launch, six at a time and in quick succession, of 360 planes from the six lurching carriers struggling to keep station in the heavy swell. The weather, already bad, had worsened as zero hour approached. On any

The Assault Force

During the first assault, 183 planes lifted off — in darkness — from the decks of six Japanese carriers. At 0705, the second wave prepared to launch. (Opposite) As the carrier *Soryu* stands by, Vals warm up on another carrier's deck. (Far left) Preparing for takeoff aboard the carrier *Shokaku*. The first plane is a Zero fighter, probably detailed to protect the carriers during the raid. (Left) *Akagi*'s signal flags flap in the breeze as maintenance crews hurry to finish readying the planes. (Below) A Kate takes off from *Shokaku*, hot on the heels of another bomber.

Rough seas continued to hamper operations as the remaining Japanese planes were readied for launching. (Below) The first plane of *Akagi's* second wave takes off. (Left) A Kate roars down *Shokaku's* deck, cheered on by watching crewmen.

"...I felt a surge of honor for being born a Japanese and serving my country."

Haruo Yoshino

Haruo Yoshino was not particularly nervous about the attack, and had no trouble eating breakfast early the morning of December 7. He and his fellow pilots were primed, thanks to the months of training they had undertaken for just this mission, and Yoshino had every confidence they would succeed.

But now he had a more immediate concern.

"The weather was bad and the sea was rough. *Kaga* pitched and rolled. I was worried about whether or not my plane, loaded with a heavy torpedo, would be able to take off."

On the departure signal, Yoshino threw open the throttle on his Kate bomber and roared down *Kaga*'s heaving flight deck.

"When I saw all the crew waving their caps, I felt a surge of honor for being born a Japanese and serving my country."

As the bomber reached the end of the ship, its wheels left the deck and the plane soared into the sky. "Despite my worries, I was able to take off successfully."

(Above) A Japanese photograph shows Val dive-bombers flying in formation. Overcast skies prompted fears among the commanders that the pilots might not be able to see their targets clearly. (Pages 62–63) Fuchida's planes fly over the coastline of Oahu.

other day, Admiral Nagumo would surely have called the whole thing off. But the first wave managed to form up, if twenty minutes later than planned, and finally headed off to the south. Six planes failed to make the first wave, marginally reducing its strength by one high-level- and three dive-bombers plus two fighters, to 183. After a short interval, the second wave began to assemble in its turn, the planes circling until every pilot found his allotted position in the disciplined swarm.

Once launched, the high-level bombers took up attack formation at 9,300 feet, with the torpedo bombers to their right at 9,148 feet and the dive-bombers to the left at 11,480. The Zeros formed a constantly shifting umbrella overall at 12,464 feet. The second wave, reduced by four to 167, formed up similarly, minus the torpedo bombers. In all, 350 planes were launched.

WHATEVER MISTAKES THE NAVY HAD MADE THAT MORNING, IT WAS THE ARMY THAT received, and fumbled, the very last advance warning. At 0400 on December 7, Privates Joseph Lockard and George Elliott had begun a three-hour shift at the SCR 270 mobile radar station located at Opana, just inland from the northernmost tip of Oahu. Sited some 230 feet above sea level, the station had been in place only two weeks. The set was temperamental but when it worked, it could pick up aircraft up to 150 miles away. As it was quiet, even for a Sunday, old radar hand Lockard was giving the greenhorn Elliott some tips on how to operate the equipment. At 0700, their shift was over and Lockard prepared to shut down prior to the theoretical training that would take up the rest of the morning. At that very moment, the oscilloscope-scanner picked up a most unusual reading — what looked like a great swarm of aircraft, easily fifty strong and approaching from a few degrees east of true north, at a range of 132 miles.

The radar stations were linked by land line to the new information center at Fort Shafter, halfway between Pearl Harbor and Honolulu. The center was built around a large "plot" of Oahu and the surrounding sea area, on which positions of aircraft reported by radar stations were shown by movable wooden pieces. Overhead was a long balcony from which a controller, an aircraft recognition officer, and other staff could survey the big picture and react if necessary. It was a Sunday so no controller was present. The only authority on hand was the duty "pursuit officer," whose job was to support the controller in guiding fighters to intercept unidentified incoming aircraft. All junior pilots took a turn at this task to learn how radar interception worked on the ground. The pursuit officer was Lieutenant Kermit Tyler, a pilot on only his second shift in the job. He too had started work at 0400, with eight enlisted men who left at 0700 when the radar was due to shut down.

Elliott phoned to report the swarm as Lockard continued to watch the screen. The switchboard operator, the only other man left on duty at the center, put the call through to Tyler just as Lockard came on the line with his latest reading on the big blip — now less than 80 miles out. On the way into work, Tyler had been listening on his car radio to KGMB, a local station, which had been playing Hawaiian music all night, something it did not normally do. The twenty-eight-year-old pilot knew why — military aircraft were coming in from the continental United States and would be using the station's output as a navigational beam. In fact, eleven Army Air Force B-17 "Flying Fortress" bombers, America's best, were due in, en route to the Philippines. They would come in from about due north. Tyler also knew that two US carriers were somewhere out to sea, but such facts were classified information and Tyler could not breach security by revealing them to Lockard. Instead, he dismissed the soldier with the words, "Well, don't worry about it."

In fairness to Tyler, Lockard did not say how big the blip was. Had he emphasized or even mentioned that he thought there were well over fifty planes, Tyler might have reacted differently in the forty-five minutes of peace that remained. The lieutenant was not punished for his failure to react — although he told interviewers long after the war that he thought he might have risen further than his ultimate rank of lieutenant colonel in the United States Air Force but for that casual payoff-line.

Radar – Hawaii's Blind Eyes

By December 1941, Oahu could boast some six portable SCR 270 mobile radar stations. But despite the success of radar in giving advance warning of attacking German planes during the Battle of Britain over a year earlier, it was still not well understood. Most senior officers knew nothing about it, skilled operators were few in number, and the often-finicky sets were in operation for only a few hours every morning — between 0400 and 0700 — when the danger of attack was thought greatest. (Above) Like an ominous warning, the towering aerial of the SCR 270 looms amid the swaying palms. (Below) An operator studies the set's oscilloscope-scanner.

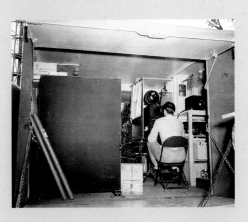

The two radar men continued to log the fascinating, looming, ever clearer blip, constantly changing shape as it approached: 0725, 62 miles; 0730, 47 miles; 0739, 22 miles. Then they lost it as the reflection from the planes merged with those from the nearby hills.

✪

FUCHIDA'S SINGLE "SURPRISE ACHIEVED" FLARE, FIRED AT 0740 OVER THE NORTHERN TIP OF Oahu, was the signal for the first wave to assume its initial attacking formation. The horizontal bombers flew steadily on at 9,840 feet while the dive-bombers climbed to 13,120. The torpedo bombers began a gentle descent that would bring them in over the harbor at battleship-deck level to attack first — before explosions, splashes, and smoke obscured their view. The fighter pilots knew they had to climb, race ahead to seize command of the air, and swoop on a plethora of targets, adding to the expected confusion on the ground. The heavy cloud cover reported by the scouts an hour earlier had begun to break up nicely. Fuchida read this as a sign from heaven.

Yet on looking up and around from the observer's seat in his Kate bomber, Fuchida realized that one large segment of the fighter cover had not reacted to his signal and must therefore not have seen it. After waiting for an agonizing ten seconds — an interval he thought long enough to forestall confusion and a false reading by pilots that surprise had not been achieved — he reopened the cockpit canopy and fired a second flare. But Takahashi read this as the signal for Plan B — no tactical surprise — and unleashed his dive-bombers first, against Ford Island and Hickam Field, the two air bases closest to Pearl Harbor.

Responding to Fuchida's radio signal, "To, to, to" — the code for "attack" — Murata, seeing no alternative, simultaneously led his torpedo bombers into their two-pronged strike against the battlefleet. The supremely complex attack plan seemed to have fallen apart before the first plane struck; but the fluffed opening was not allowed to detract from the overall performance.

The high-level and torpedo planes swung across the north coast of Oahu from the northeast and then around the westward and southward sides of the island, the torpedo bombers on the inside. One group of the latter flew in on Pearl Harbor from a southeasterly direction while the high-levels came in from the southwest. The other group of torpedo bombers diverged to attack the anchorage from the north. The fighters flew from the north down the broad central valley between the two parallel mountain ranges on either side of the island, the various groups peeling off with graceful precision to shoot up the air bases.

Fuchida next sent the immortal codeword that all the Japanese units, involved in the highly intricate, multiple southward advance in the Far East, were awaiting: "Tora, tora, tora!" The word means "tiger"; the signal told Nagumo, who relayed it to Japan for forwarding to all forces, that total strategic and tactical surprise had been achieved over Oahu. Countless other operations against Malaya, the Philippines, and the Dutch East Indies could therefore go ahead. Bad weather on Formosa grounded the Japanese air forces there and saved the Philippines, but only for half a day. There would be no interference from a United States battlefleet. Local time was 0753.

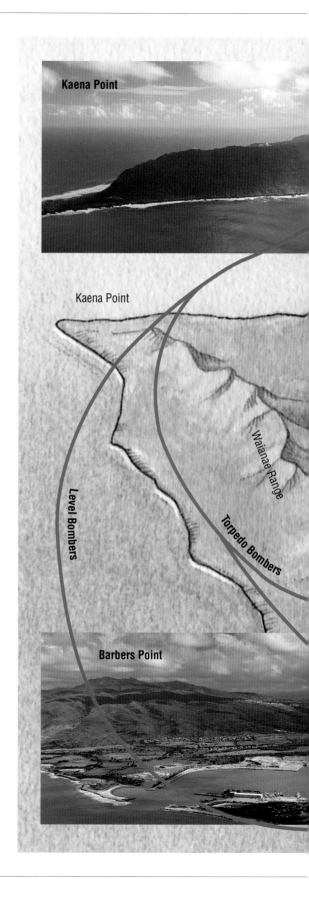

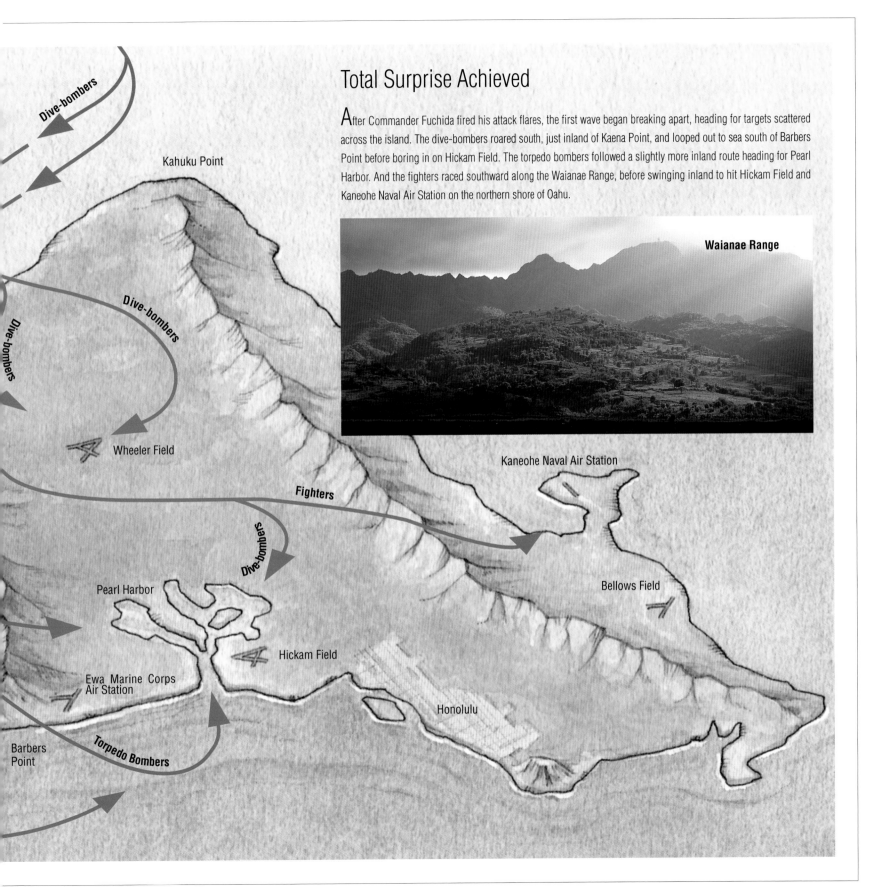

Total Surprise Achieved

After Commander Fuchida fired his attack flares, the first wave began breaking apart, heading for targets scattered across the island. The dive-bombers roared south, just inland of Kaena Point, and looped out to sea south of Barbers Point before boring in on Hickam Field. The torpedo bombers followed a slightly more inland route heading for Pearl Harbor. And the fighters raced southward along the Waianae Range, before swinging inland to hit Hickam Field and Kaneohe Naval Air Station on the northern shore of Oahu.

Waianae Range

Dive-bombers

Dive-bombers

Dive-bombers

Kahuku Point

Wheeler Field

Fighters

Kaneohe Naval Air Station

Dive-bombers

Bellows Field

Pearl Harbor

Hickam Field

Ewa Marine Corps Air Station

Honolulu

Barbers Point

Torpedo Bombers

Part Two THIS IS NO DRILL!

CHAPTER FOUR

The Shock of Battle

"We heard what sounded [like] low-flying planes and explosions, but as the air station was still under construction, didn't really pay attention to it, though someone commented on the fact they were working on Sunday."

— Marine Private First Class James Evans

At the Kaneohe Naval Air Station, Marine Private First Class James Evans was waiting in the base barracks for a truck to take him to the main gate, where he was to stand guard from 0800 to noon, as eleven Zeros of the first wave roared in.

> Suddenly someone came running into the barracks yelling, "We're being attacked by the Japs!" Panic prevailed as we scrambled for our rifles; ammunition was another story. The storeroom was locked and it took a few minutes to find the supply sergeant and get him to issue ammo without the proper authority.
>
> A couple of us took a water-cooled machine gun up to the second deck [storey] of the barracks; we planned to mount the gun on the roof, as we would have an excellent field of fire on the planes banking around the barracks. One of the [men] boosted me up to the ladder leading to the roof. When I opened the hatch and stuck my head through, here comes a Jap plane so close that I could see the pilot's teeth as he grinned at me. I'll never forget that. We made eye contact.
>
> When I realized there was nothing but training ammunition for the machine gun, I loaded my rifle and braced myself on the ladder, with my elbows on the roof, and got off five rounds. From my perch on the roof, I had a great view of the action down by the hangars and the seaplane ramp — Jap Zeros strafing the PBYs moored in the bay and on the ramps. I could see the tracer bullets from the planes and from the ground, as the sailors were returning the fire by now. Everything down there seemed to be burning.
>
> I left my perch on the ladder as I soon realized that I wasn't going to hit a plane going a couple hundred miles an hour with an '03 rifle. I went down to the second deck and joined the rest of the marines firing at the planes through the windows. We had a good field of fire as the planes banked past the row of barracks after strafing the seaplane ramp and hangar area.

Kaneohe was the home of Naval Patrol Wing One, consisting of three squadrons of twelve twin-engined PBY Catalina flying boats. Three aircraft were on routine patrol west of Oahu at the time; four were floating at their moorings in the bay, about 1,000 yards apart; four were inside hangar number one; the rest, twenty-five in all, were on the ramp. One plane was on ready duty with its crew. A total of thirty Navy maintenance men and other personnel were also on hand. After only a few seconds of fire from the Zeros' 20mm cannon and machine guns, the station erupted in flames.

The aircraft lined up on the ramp were immolated by their own blazing fuel. Twenty-

(Left) Amid the heavy smoke, sailors at Kaneohe Naval Air Station struggle to push a PBY flying boat to safety.
(Pages 66–67) The first wave of Japanese planes swoops down on Hickam Field.

Japanese bombs destroyed twenty-seven PBYs at Kaneohe and damaged six, catching them parked on the concrete launch ramps or moored in the bay. (Below left) A cab filled with sailors races to Kaneohe. (Below right) Firefighters struggle to douse a blazing flying boat.

"I remember my mother's voice as she pulled me back inside, 'It's on the radio. It's war!'"

Peter Nottage

Thirteen-year-old Peter Nottage witnessed the attack on the naval air station from a high bluff on the other side of Kaneohe Bay. He and his family were spending the weekend with friends and he'd gotten up early to go exploring.

"I had barely reached a good lookout point when I heard a drone behind me. I looked up in time to see three silvery planes coming in from the west — right over the house! — and so low I could see the goggled faces of the pilots and the big red circles on the wings."

Peter figured all the activity overhead was probably some sort of training exercise. The planes swooped in over the bay, spraying the water with machine-gun fire. Then a bomb dropped on the seaplane ramp and one of the planes at anchor exploded.

"Smoke and flames were everywhere," he recalled. "It looked like all the seaplanes were on fire and the hangars, too."

seven planes at the station, which had no antiaircraft guns, were destroyed and six damaged as the Zeros stormed back and forth at will. Only the three on patrol were unscathed. The fact that only eighteen men were killed in the pandemonium on the ground seems remarkable in retrospect. Men risked, and sometimes lost, their lives in vain attempts to save the planes. Naval Aviation Chief Ordnanceman John Finn was awarded the Congressional Medal of Honor for his heroic resistance, continuing to fire at the Japanese despite being wounded.

✪

AT 0755, NINE JAPANESE DIVE-BOMBERS SWOOPED DOWN ON FORD ISLAND. THEIR MISSION: TO prevent retaliation by destroying as many American planes as possible. A navy nurse, Lieutenant Ruth Erickson, had just got up after working the 3 P.M. to 10 P.M. shift the night before at the naval hospital just across the water to the south of Ford.

John Finn (above) won the Medal of Honor for manning a machine gun at Kaneohe despite being surrounded by burning gasoline and receiving a shot through one heel. (Right) The main naval air station at Ford Island was hit hard by dive-bombers during the first wave.

Two or three of us were sitting in the dining room Sunday morning having a late breakfast and talking over coffee. Suddenly we heard planes roaring overhead and we said, "The fly-boys are really busy at Ford Island this morning."

I leaped out of my chair and dashed to the nearest window in the corridor. Right then, there was a plane flying directly over the top of our quarters, a one-storey structure. The rising sun under the wing of the plane denoted the enemy. One could almost see [the pilot's] features around his goggles. He was obviously saving his ammunition for the ships.

My heart was racing, the telephone was ringing, the chief nurse, Gertrude Arnest, was saying, "Girls, get into your uniforms at once. This is the real thing!"

On Ford Island, Ted LeBaron was looking forward to a relatively relaxed Sunday — and also to his twenty-first birthday, which was just eighteen days away, on Christmas Day. He had joined naval patrol squadron VP 22 just over a year earlier as a maintenance man specializing in bombsights. He came out onto the lanai of his wing's quarters as he struggled into his uniform.

At that moment, I heard an explosion. When I looked up, I could see a cloud of black smoke in the area of our hangar. I did not see the plane because it had apparently already climbed above the overhang of the floor above.

I did see the second plane make his drop at the same location but I was looking at the rear of the plane, so no way to make any identification. At this moment, there was a commotion on the lanai on the opposite side of our wing. I ran the thirty or so feet over to that side to see what the yelling was about. Looking up, but not very far up, I was looking at a Jap pilot in an open-cockpit torpedo plane who was waving at us! That first torpedo plane I saw had just finished his run on the USS California.

I have no idea how long it took me to get to the hangar. It involved going a few feet, then ducking for cover either when I heard a lot of shrapnel or when a dive-bomber would drop one on the Nevada, *which was then directly abreast of me.*

When I did get to the hangar, I think nearly all our planes were gutted from the burning of the gas in the wings. Right as I arrived at the hangar, one of the planes from the Enterprise *was trying to land. Because of some itchy trigger-fingers, the plane was being fired on by some of our men. I remember that the guy on duty in our hangar at the time of the bombing was firing his .45 at this plane. I was yelling at him to stop but he would have shot at anything with wings — he was maniacal about wanting to get even right then and completely frustrated by having only a .45 pistol, since all our machine guns had been destroyed by fire during the bombing.*

Hangar 6 at the southeast end of Ford Island was hardest hit, shattered by perhaps five bombs that wrecked the seaplane ramp and set many planes on fire. Hangar 38 was also damaged. One 550-pound bomb with a delayed-action fuse buried itself in the ground outside the dispensary, blowing a large crater but injuring no one. Firefighters were reduced to pumping up water from the artesian well on the island when the 12-inch water main from the mainland was struck and blocked. A bomb also severed the subsidiary 6-inch underwater pipeline to the southern end of Ford. Thirty-three planes out of seventy on the island at the time were destroyed or damaged. Miraculously, only one man was killed and twenty-five injured.

Lieutenant Commander Logan Ramsey, operations officer of Patrol Wing Two, was at the island command center when the raid began. He raced over to the radio room and ordered the operator to transmit in plain language the electrifying message, "Air raid Pearl Harbor! This is no drill!" It bore the signature of Rear Admiral Patrick Bellinger, the commander of Patrol Wing Two. It was as if the suddenly beleaguered garrison of Oahu was collectively pinching itself to make sure it was not dreaming. Although few bore the urgency of Chief Boatswain's Mate Fred Ketchum, on the appropriately named USS *Blue* (who roused his men by bellowing, "All hands man your battle stations! We are being bombed by the Japs and this is no shit!"), the endless calls, "The real thing! no drill! not drill! the real McCoy!," occurred time and again in the messages that flashed around the

The seaplane ramp at
Ford Island after the attack.

(Above) Several hangars at Ford Island were burned out or damaged. (Below) One of Ford Island's hangars today. The milky-paned windows are originals that survived the raid intact.

fleet, the air bases and barracks, and then to a worldwide audience. Within minutes, people in Washington, all of America, and the world at large were reeling at the enormity of what was happening in the middle of the Pacific.

When Bellinger's message was handed to Navy Secretary Frank Knox in Washington minutes after the raid began, he said: "My God, this can't be true, this must mean the Philippines!" In shock, Knox picked up the phone to inform the rest of the administration.

✪

IT HAD BEEN A LATE NIGHT AT THE JAPANESE EMBASSY. SENSING THAT THEIR TIME IN Washington was short, the depleted staff had gone on a bit of a binge.

Now, head throbbing, one of the few junior diplomatic clerks left at the embassy was doing hunt and peck at a typewriter. The previous day, the embassy had received a thirteen-part message (also intercepted and decoded by the Americans) restating that the junta would not yield to American demands. On Sunday morning, the fourteenth part of the message came through — along with instructions that Ambassador Nomura deliver the translated message to American Secretary of State Cordell Hull no later than 1 P.M. Washington time.

Nomura set the clerk to typing, to produce a fair copy of the dispatch that he could hand to Hull. But it was taking far longer than expected. Nomura phoned the Americans, putting off his meeting until 2 P.M.

Unknown to Nomura, the original time set for the delivery of his laboriously transcribed document (1 P.M. in Washington, 7:30 A.M. in Hawaii) had been intended to anticipate the start of the raid by exactly half an hour. The junta fondly imagined that this simplistic stratagem would enable them to split hairs and claim that they had not acted without warning (even so, the message contained no declaration of war but only broke off diplomatic relations). But the ambassador was sixty-five minutes late when he bowed from the waist and handed over the paper at 2:05 P.M.

Meanwhile, 5,000 miles to the west, Fuchida's pilots had managed to make up time after their launch delays, enabling him to start the attack seven minutes early, at 7:53 A.M. Hawaiian time (1:23 P.M. in Washington). Nomura was therefore running forty-two minutes behind events instead of thirty minutes ahead.

America's senior diplomat had just come off the phone as Nomura entered. Quivering with shock and rage, Hull merely glanced at the laboriously prepared note before laying into the Japanese ambassador:

> *In all my fifty years of public service, I have never seen such a document that was more crowded with infamous falsehoods and distortions on a scale so huge that I never imagined until today that any government on this planet was capable of uttering them.*

Wordlessly, he gestured to Nomura to shut up and go. Perhaps the envoy wondered how Hull knew the contents of a document he had not read. But Nomura only found out what was going on — and how he had been cynically deceived by his own masters — on his return to the embassy.

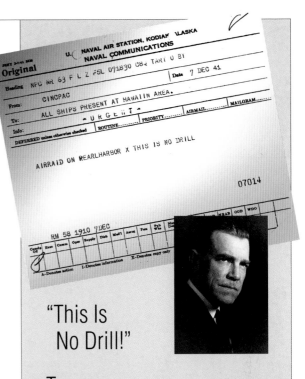

"This Is No Drill!"

The first message about the attack was sent out by radio operators working for Ford Island's commander, Rear Admiral Patrick Bellinger (above). The commander in chief of the Pacific fleet (CINCPAC) fired off a similar message (top) alerting American naval stations as far afield as Alaska. Bellinger's warning was the first news of the raid to reach Washington, just before an unsuspecting Ambassador Nomura (below, far left) was to meet American Secretary of State Cordell Hull to discuss Japan's latest diplomatic ultimatum.

CHAPTER FIVE

The First Wave

"...even after I saw a huge fireball and cloud
of black smoke rise from the hangars on
Ford Island and heard explosions, it did not
occur to me that these were enemy planes."

— Lee Soucy, Pharmacist's Mate Second Class on USS *Utah*

THE TWO GROUPS OF TORPEDO BOMBERS EXECUTED A PINCER MOVEMENT ON FORD ISLAND, sixteen coming in directly from the northwest while twenty-four swung around Oahu to fly in over Hickam Field from the southeast. The pilots of the smaller group were bitterly disappointed to see no carriers in place. The only armed ships on the northwestern side were the light cruisers *Detroit* and *Raleigh* and the old battleship *Utah* — which some pilots mistook for a carrier. (This was because of the disarmed battlewagon's mooring position, the fact she had no heavy guns, and the heavy timbers laid on her main deck as protection against dummy bombs used in target practice.) Despite orders to save their torpedoes for major targets, six planes launched at these ships.

One torpedo struck the *Raleigh* forward of amidships and below the bridge on the port side, flooding the forward engine room just as the ship's antiaircraft gun crews were turning out for what they thought was an exercise against a mock attack. They at least had immediate access to ready ammunition, which was not the case on many other ships. Captain Bentham Simons was aboard and directed frantic efforts to save the ship from capsizing by counter-flooding and throwing every possible weighty object overboard as she listed heavily to port.

Utah, hit in quick succession by two torpedoes, began immediately listing heavily to port. Pharmacist's Mate Second Class Lee Soucy, in the sick bay after breakfast, was amazed by what he saw through a porthole:

When I looked up in the sky I saw five or six planes starting their descent. Then when the first bombs dropped on the hangars at Ford Island, I thought, "Those guys are missing us by a mile."

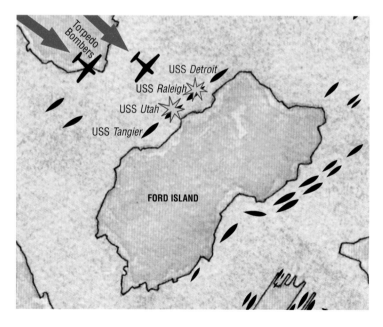

(Pages 78–79) As smoke from the destruction on Ford Island fills the sky, USS *Oglala* lies capsized at 1010 dock. (Map) The pilots who flew in over the north side of Ford Island were disappointed that no carriers were moored there. Despite instructions to save torpedoes for important targets, six of the sixteen bombers launched at *Raleigh* and *Utah*. (Right) Mortally wounded by two torpedoes, *Utah* starts rolling over.

(Below) Within minutes, *Utah* had capsized completely. Today, the wreck (above), which was rolled back partially upright to move it out of the ship channel, still sits off Ford Island — a poignant reminder of the grim toll of December 7, 1941.

(Above) A badly damaged *Raleigh*, kept afloat by barges carrying large buoyancy tanks, sits to the left of the overturned *Utah*. (Inset) Pharmacist's Mate Second Class Lee Soucy, shown here in a later photograph, slid down *Utah*'s hull as she capsized. Fifty-eight of his shipmates didn't survive the strike on the *Utah*. (Right) The medic's armband Soucy was wearing the morning of the attack.

It occurred to me and to most of the others that someone had really goofed this time and put live bombs on those planes by mistake. In any event, even after I saw a huge fireball and cloud of black smoke rise from the hangars on Ford Island and heard explosions, it did not occur to me that these were enemy planes.

I felt the ship lurch. The bugler and boatswain's mate were on the fantail ready to raise the colors at eight o'clock. In a matter of seconds, the bugler sounded "General Quarters." As I was running down the passageway toward my battle station, another torpedo hit and shook the ship severely. I was knocked off balance and through the log-room door. By then, the ship was already listing. After a minute or two below the armored deck, we heard another bugle call, then the boatswain's whistle followed by the boatswain's chant, "Abandon ship! Abandon ship!"

After sliding down the barnacle-encrusted side of the capsizing ship, Soucy found himself swimming toward a launch.

After a few strokes, a hail of bullets hit the water a few feet in front of me in line with the launch. As the strafer banked, I noticed the big red insignia on his wing tips. Until then I really had not known who attacked us. At some point I had heard someone shout, "Where did those Germans come from?" I changed course and hightailed it for Ford Island. I reached the beach exhausted and as I tried to catch my breath, another pharmacist's mate from the Utah, *Gordon Sumner, stumbled out of the water. I remember how elated I was to see him.*

Mess Attendant Clark B. Simmons helped some officers escape through a porthole before wriggling free himself. All told, fifty-eight men lost their lives on the *Utah* that day. Chief Water Tender Peter Tomich was awarded the Medal of Honor posthumously for his selfless efforts to save others on the old ship.

✪

FIVE AIRCRAFT FROM THE SMALLER GROUP OF KATES ROARED ACROSS FORD Island, one of them launching its torpedo at two ships moored in tandem outside the western wall of 1010 dock, at the northern extremity of the Navy Yard. The outboard vessel was the minelayer *Oglala*, so old that in the usually affectionate eyes of her crew she looked like a wreck anyway. Even so, she was the flagship of Rear Admiral William Furlong, who commanded the service vessels of the Pacific Fleet and was that day's Senior Officer Present Afloat. In fact, he was pacing the quarterdeck at 0755 awaiting his late Sunday breakfast when a bomber pulled out of its dive on Ford Island almost in front of his nose. Recognizing the red roundel on the wings, Furlong reacted immmediately with two orders — to his flagship, "General Quarters," and to the fleet, "All ships in harbor: sortie."

"I will always maintain that God and my Guardian Angel pointed that long timber toward me."

Clarence Durham

Radioman Third Class Clarence Durham was in the radio room's sleeping compartment when he was tossed out of bed. Almost immediately, the USS *Utah* began to tilt rapidly. Durham's closest escape route — the airshaft off the radio room — was blocked by an iron grate that had broken loose. Another lower grate was blocking any escape from the engine room below.

"I never forgot the faces of those men trapped in the engine room," Durham said. "I knew there was no way I could lift those steel grates." And the ship continued to roll over.

Durham ran through the radio room to the airshaft on the opposite side and crawled through. He reached daylight and managed to crawl onto the ship's bottom just before the massive battleship turned over. Once in the water, Durham found himself being sucked downward.

"I would have drowned then and there had it not been that a piece of heavy timber floated within reach and I grabbed onto it."

"The American reaction was so swift."

Yuji Akamatsu

Torpedo bomber observer Yuji Akamatsu was one of the *Kaga* airmen in the first wave's torpedo attack. Only minutes after crossing the shoreline of Oahu, the bomber group had formed up, then roared on toward Pearl Harbor. Following their leader, Akamatsu's plane flew in low and launched at the battleship *California*, moored close to *Neosho* and just across the harbor from the minelayer *Oglala*.

As his plane pulled away shortly after the attack had begun, the young airman "flew into a fierce counter-attack. It looked as if all the fire was aimed at my plane. I had never been so scared."

Although Akamatsu's Kate successfully dodged the American antiaircraft fire, others were not so lucky. Five planes from his squadron were shot down — along with fifteen of his friends.

Akamatsu remembered how painful that first night back on the *Kaga* was. "I felt so sad and lonely to see all the empty beds. They were everywhere — above me, to my right and left."

Thanks to the minelayer's shallow draft, the torpedo passed under his ship. It struck the USS *Helena*, a light cruiser inboard of her that lay deeper in the water. Chief Petty Officer Leonard J. Fox was aboard, writing a letter to his wife and daughter in Phoenix, Arizona, at 0756 when he heard low-flying aircraft and went out onto the main deck to watch the enemy planes attacking a wide range of targets. He could see bombs raining down on Ford Island.

A Jap plane spied the Helena. *He made a fast turn and headed our way. He was only about a hundred yards away when he released his torpedo. A tremendous shuddering took place and billowing smoke and flame shut all the sunlight out of my life and I believed my ship was no more.*

The blast of the torpedo that hit the *Helena*, flooding her engine room, also caused enormous damage to her neighbor *Oglala*, breaking her back. To avoid more damage to the cruiser, the minelayer was moved by tugs to a position astern, where she capsized two hours later. The *Helena* remained on an even keel, firing her antiaircraft guns throughout the rest of the raid.

The fleet oiler *Neosho* had tied up in the middle of Battleship Row on Saturday the 6th, carrying a cargo of highly explosive aviation fuels for Ford Island. She had just finished unloading it minutes before the attack. With her tanks still full of vapor, a bomb hit might easily have set off the fuel stores ashore and added to the woes of the battleships nearby. Commander John Phillips was able to send up a hail of antiaircraft fire as he got her under way within minutes.

The torpedo that hit the light cruiser USS *Helena* (top), caused relatively minor damage — but the blast from it broke the back of the minelayer *Oglala* (above) moored next to her, and (opposite) she capsized two hours after the raid.

Fires rage at Hickam Field shortly after a devastating ten-minute assault by Japanese planes.

SEVENTEEN VAL DIVE-BOMBERS AND EIGHTEEN ZEROS OF THE first wave hit Hickam Field, the principal base of the Hawaiian Air Force (HAF), south of the Navy Yard. The raiders arrived at 0755 and blasted the air base for ten terrible minutes. Hickam Field was the scene of the US Army's heaviest casualties in the raid.

Colonel William E. Farthing, the commander of the Fifth Bomb Group, was in the control tower early that Sunday morning. So were Lieutenant Colonel Cheney Bertholf, adjutant general of the HAF, and Captain Gordon Blake, the operations officer at Hickam. Lieutenant Colonel James A. Mollison, HAF chief of staff, had just phoned to say he was on his way. The high turnout of "brass" was there to see the eleven B-17s arrive from California.

To facilitate their long journey, the planes were unarmed and they would have little fuel left on landing. Everything was squared away on the surrounding tarmac apron: twelve B-17s, thirty-three obsolete B-18s of the Eighteenth Bombardment Wing, and twelve A-20 attack bombers neatly lined up, wingtips just ten feet apart in four parallel rows about 130 feet apart — to make life as easy as possible for the lightly armed guards protecting the planes from harm. Ammunition and aircraft machine guns were securely locked away for fear of saboteurs.

The Japanese swooped down from the north. Dive-bombers, their fixed landing gear making them look like giant birds of prey with outstretched talons, screamed down just before 0800, hitting the conveniently bunched aircraft, the two runways, a double row of ten hangars, the Hawaiian Air Depot with its workshops and offices, the parachute store, the armory, the waterworks, the barracks, the post exchange, and the mess hall. Simultaneously, two groups of nine Zeros roared in from southeast and southwest, sometimes at rooftop level, peppering scores of targets with their machine guns and cannon. Not even the

chapel was spared. Sergeant Nick Gaynos, who had been on duty all night in the radio building waiting for the B-17s and was returning to barracks at 0745, recalled:

All hell broke loose with the strafing of the wooden barracks by Zeros. I commandeered a weapons carrier with a mounted .50 caliber gun and raced down Hangar Avenue toward my radio transmitter building on the ball field. The hangar line was ablaze with aircraft and fuel trucks, and smoke was belching from the hangars. I remember seeing bodies and walking wounded as I raced up the street and also briefly firing the machine gun with questionable results. The chaos and pandemonium of the first wave created an open season on all targets with constant low-level strafing and bombing.

Targeting Hickam

The seventeen Val dive-bombers and eighteen Zero fighters that hit Hickam Field during the first raid caused extensive damage and destroyed numerous parked aircraft, including this shattered B-17 (below). Facilities at the base were hit hard, too, including the fire hall (opposite, left), which was heavily strafed by machine-gun fire. Today, it serves as the base police station (opposite, top right). Hickam's large block of barracks also took its share of punishment (right), and bullet holes are still evident in the building today (opposite, bottom right).

Although Hickam was only hit for ten minutes during the first strike, 182 men were killed or missing — the US Army's heaviest casualties in the raid.

Colonel Mollison was halfway through shaving at his quarters at Hickam when the attack began. Throwing on a minimum of clothes, he rushed to the HAF offices and phoned Colonel Walter Phillips, General Short's chief of staff, to report the bombardment. Phillips had heard the explosions and was still mystified, unable to believe it was a surprise enemy attack: "You must be out of your mind!" he told Mollison. Then, doing his best to come to terms with the awful truth, he promised to send over a liaison officer. In fact, Major General Frederick L. Martin himself arrived, sick to his stomach (literally; he suffered from ulcers, which were now playing up ferociously). The HAF commander's only thought was to get bombers into the air to counterattack the Japanese carriers, wherever they might be. He phoned Admiral Bellinger, commanding naval land-based aviation, to coordinate a search for the attackers and eventually managed to get four Army B-17s into the air.

Into the middle of the attack at Hickam flew an exhausted Major Truman Landon, at the controls of a B-17, the first of the eleven coming in from California. With minimal crews and almost out of fuel after fourteen hours in the air, the big bombers had no choice but to set down in the midst of the battle. Landon was at first pleasantly surprised to see a flight of pursuit planes apparently coming out to welcome him, then horrified as he began his approach to the burning air base from the north with three Zeros trying to shoot him down. Hotly pursued, all eleven unarmed planes managed to land — most at Hickam, but one reached Bellows Field and another touched down at a golf course on the north side of Oahu.

(Above) These Japanese Val bombers were photographed from one of the B-17s flying in to Hickam Field that morning from California. (Right) Crewmen sort through luggage from a B-17 after its hasty landing at the base.

THE FIRST BOMB OF THE RAID FELL ON WHEELER FIELD, THE HAWAIIAN AIR FORCE'S MAIN fighter base, at 0751, just before Fuchida's triumphant, coded tally-ho announcing that surprise had been achieved. Base commander Colonel William Flood had hoped to disperse his 153 aircraft, including 87 of the latest P-40s, in horseshoe-shaped earthen bunkers. But his suggestion had been overruled, lest it upset the civilian population. Twenty-five Val dive-bombers led by Lieutenant Akira Sakamoto roared past Kolekole Pass and destroyed most of Wheeler's planes in a murderous quarter of an hour. Escorted by eight strafing Zeros, the bombers came down so low that two flew back to their ship with telephone wires dangling from their wheels. Staff Sergeant George Sallick was a member of the ground crew of the Nineteenth Fighter Squadron:

I got out about five yards from the porch when a bomb hit just about where Sergeant Guthrie was. I didn't hear it but saw the tree between the bomb and me turn gray and shake. I thought the bomb hit the tree. When I regained consciousness, I was lying on my stomach and facing toward the barracks, looking at my tin hat with the top cut off. I was covered with blood and several men fainted when they saw me. I waited fourteen hours to get my wounds attended to.

Out of all the P-40s at Wheeler Field, it took an entire week to assemble seven planes from the salvaged parts of destroyed planes.

Probably Sergeant Guthrie was the first American killed in World War II and I [was] the first wounded.

✪

THE US MARINE CORPS HAD FORTY-EIGHT AIRCRAFT AT ITS LONE AIR BASE ON OAHU, AT EWA in the southwest — including twenty-three of the new Dauntless SBD dive-bombers and F4F fighters — all in the three squadrons of the Twenty-First Marine Aircraft Group. As descending Japanese torpedo bombers passed insouciantly low overhead, six Zeros came in at 0753 to strafe the airfield with its 5,000-foot runway. Base commander Lieutenant Colonel Claude Larkin was shot up in his car on his way to the airfield. He dived unscathed into a ditch for cover but was hit by shrapnel later in the raid.

(Left) Wheeler Field, home to most of Oahu's fighter squadrons, was hit early in the raid and most of the island's fighter defenses were destroyed before they ever had a chance to get in the air. (Inset) Today, Wheeler serves as the base for various Army helicopter squadrons. (Right) Japanese fighters downed this Navy SBD dive-bomber near the Marines' Ewa Field.

CHAPTER SIX

Battleship Row

"Torpedo planes swooped on from almost over my head and started toward Battleship Row, dropping their lethal fish. Men were soon swimming for their lives in the fire-covered waters of Pearl Harbor."

— Leonard J. Fox, Chief Petty Officer, USS *Helena*

IF THE PEARL HARBOR ATTACK WAS AN EARTHQUAKE, AS SOME WHO FELT THE EXPLOSIONS might first have thought, then Battleship Row was its epicenter. Armed with massive 14- or 16-inch guns, bristling with a secondary armament of dual-purpose 5-inch and smaller guns, and protected by a belt of heavy armor around their vitals, the battlewagons moored there were the pride of the United States Navy. But after eighty years of dominating naval strategy, the glory of the armored line-of-battle ship as queen of the seas was about to come to an end.

At 0755, the signal tower at the center of the Navy Yard hoisted the "Blue Peter," the blue-bordered white signal flag representing the letter P. The signal was a reminder to all ships to get ready for colors — the ceremony of hoisting the Stars and Stripes at the stern, at 0800. On the *Arizona*, as on others, an honor guard of marines stood at attention awaiting the order to hoist the ensign. When they heard the first explosions on Ford Island, they quickly raised the flag and rushed to their battle stations. The first torpedo struck the *West Virginia*; several more would follow, sending her to the shallow bottom.

The second torpedo hit the *Oklahoma*. Lieutenant Jinichi Goto, leader of the torpedo-bomber squadron from the *Akagi*, came in so low with two other planes, at sixty-six feet, that he almost hit the battleship's crow's nest from underneath as he pulled out of his shallow dive. "My observer reported a huge waterspout springing up from the ship's position. '*Atarimashita!*' he cried" — the crewman's way of telling the world that their plane had

These photographs, taken from Japanese bombers, document the opening moments of the attack on Battleship Row. (Left) A geyser of water marks a near miss. (Above) Torpedo tracks head for the battleships *West Virginia*, where a shock wave from a hit is visible, and *Oklahoma*.

"...an explosion took place, and then another one, and another one.... The ship started to turn over almost immediately....The machinery on the deck started to shift and began falling against the bulkheads."

— George DeLong, Quartermaster Striker, USS *Oklahoma*

FORD ISLAND

USS *Arizona*   USS *Nevada*
USS *Tennessee*   USS *Vestal*
USS *Maryland*   USS *West Virginia*
USS *Neosho*   USS *Oklahoma*
USS *California*

USS *Pennsylvania*

Torpedo and Level Bombers

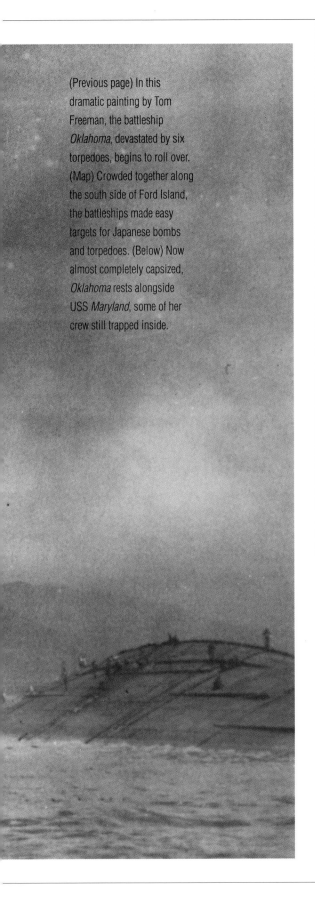

(Previous page) In this dramatic painting by Tom Freeman, the battleship *Oklahoma*, devastated by six torpedoes, begins to roll over. (Map) Crowded together along the south side of Ford Island, the battleships made easy targets for Japanese bombs and torpedoes. (Below) Now almost completely capsized, *Oklahoma* rests alongside USS *Maryland*, some of her crew still trapped inside.

scored a direct hit. His target had eight minutes left to live, during which many more torpedoes would strike home. The *Oklahoma*'s executive officer, Commander J.L. Kenworthy, took charge in the absence ashore of the captain, ordering the crew to abandon ship via the starboard side as she began to heel over to port. Her masts jammed in the shallow harbor floor and stopped her turning full circle, but the ship's bottom was fully exposed.

Father Aloysius Schmitt was on the second deck, below the main deck, with more than one hundred other men when the ship turned over. Schmitt, who had been in the Navy just two and a half years, led them, first in prayer, then up an inverted ladder to the second deck, then to the third as the water filled the hull. Finally, when he could climb no farther, he found a small compartment with a watertight door. He ushered as many men into the air pocket as it would take and then fastened the door — from the outside. The men within were among those saved after the raid: rescuers cut their way into the hull of the ship with welding torches the next day in response to frantic banging from inside.

Other survivors related how, in a compartment where only a small porthole provided outlet for escape, Schmitt unselfishly helped his shipmates through the aperture. When they, in turn, tried to pull him through, his body became wedged in the narrow opening. At the same time, Schmitt realized that other men had come into the compartment looking for a way out. He told his would-be rescuers to push him back into the ship so that the others might try to get through the opening. Calmly urging them on with a blessing, he remained behind while they crawled out to safety.

Some of those Schmitt saved thought that something in his pocket had prevented the priest from wriggling through the porthole — it may have been his Roman Catholic breviary or else the flask of holy oil he needed for giving the last rites to the dying. Schmitt's breviary was recovered when the *Oklahoma* was righted in December 1943. The marker for the day's holy office for December 7, 1941, was still in place. The priest's body, however, was never found.

No one knows whether Schmitt or his Presbyterian colleague, Rev. T.L. Kirkpatrick, on the *Arizona* at the time, died first. But the two were the first American chaplains of their respective denominations killed in the war, and only the second and third to die in action in the history of the United States Navy. Father Schmitt was awarded a US Navy and Marine Corps Medal posthumously. A destroyer escort named after him was launched by one of his sisters in 1943.

(Right) Salvaged from the *Oklahoma* in the cleanup after the attack, this watch stopped at the moment the battleship rolled over, as water flooded the hull. (Overleaf) The fatal bomb drops on USS *Arizona*.

NO TORPEDOES STRUCK THE *ARIZONA*, MOORED INBOARD OF THE REPAIR SHIP *VESTAL*, which paid heavily for the unsought honor of a temporary berth among the battlewagons. Instead, that battleship, over 600 feet long and armed with twelve 14-inch guns, was targeted by the high-level Kates, each carrying one 1,760-pound battleship shell specially adapted to penetrate armored decks. Captain Franklin Van Valkenburgh had time to order General Quarters and the air-raid alarms sounded as he raced to the bridge to try to save his ship. Four bombs struck home, the first by the aftermost main turret, number four.

Unfortunately, the last, likely dropped by a Kate from *Hiryu*, struck at 0810 beside turret number two forward, plunging deep into the ship not far from Seaman Second Class George Phraner's post:

> My battle station was on a forward 5-inch gun. There we were, the Japanese dropping bombs over us and we had no ammo. All the training and practising for a year and when the real thing came, we had no ammunition. As unfortunate as this was, that simple fact was to save my life. Somehow the gun captain pointed at me and said, "You go aft and start bringing up the ammunition out of the magazines."

> I had begun lifting [90-pound] shells into the hoist when a deafening roar filled the room and the entire ship shuddered. It was the forward magazine. [Fifty tons] of gunpowder exploding in a massive fireball disintegrating the whole forward part of the ship. Only moments before, I [had] stood with my gun crew just a few feet from the center of the explosion.

> The lights went out and it was pitch black; a thick, acrid smoke filled the magazine locker and the metal walls began to get hot. Somehow we were able to open the hatch and start to make our way up the ladder. I was nauseated by the smell of burning flesh, which turned out to be my own as I climbed up the hot ladder. Getting through that choking kind of smoke was a real ordeal. After a while I began to get weak and light-headed. I could feel myself losing the battle to save my own life. At that moment, I looked up and could see a small point of light through the smoke. It gave me the strength to go on. After what seemed to me like an eternity, I reached the deck gasping and choking. I lay down for a few moments. The warm Hawaiian air filled my lungs and cleared my head. I glanced over to the forward end of the ship to see nothing but a giant wall of flame and smoke.

> Behind me a marine lay dead on the deck, his body split in two. I began to realize there were dead men all around me. Some men were burning, wandering aimlessly. It was obvious the ship was doomed. I made my way to the side of the ship, which by this time was sinking fast, and jumped off the fantail. The shoreline of Ford Island was only a short distance. There was burning oil all around the ship, but the aft was clear.

"...a deafening roar filled the room and the entire ship shuddered. It was the forward magazine. [Fifty tons] of gunpowder exploding in a massive fireball. ..."

— George Phraner,
Seaman Second Class, USS *Arizona*

(Below) In this rare color still taken from film shot during the attack on Pearl Harbor, *Arizona*'s forward magazine explodes. (Right, top to bottom) The explosion literally tore the ship open, causing her forward control tower to tilt precipitously. Despite flooding, she continued to burn for many hours after being hit.

*"We choked on the smell of fuel oil
and the terrible odor of burnt flesh."*

Edward Johann

From the deck of the USS *Solace*, a hospital ship moored at the north end of Ford Island, Seaman Ed Johann and his shipmates observed the devastation on Battleship Row with mounting horror. "All around us ships were taking a horrible beating," he remembered. "Everywhere there was turmoil and confusion. It was inhuman and grotesque."

He and two others jumped into one of the ship's motor launches and headed toward the burning *Arizona* to see if they could help.

"The water was filled with floating debris, and the planes kept diving down out of the sun."

Long after the attackers had gone, Johann and his shipmates continued their errand of mercy. Each time they pulled the launch alongside a stricken ship, injured men were lowered down to them "until the boat was loaded with the wounded, all pressed together, all in great pain."

With each trip, the task became more gruesome as the air around them filled with the sounds of men moaning and screaming, shipboard explosions, flames and thick black smoke — and the unforgettable smell of burnt flesh.

George Phraner survived but the *Arizona*'s captain and Rear Admiral Isaac C. Kidd, commander of Battleship Division One, were less fortunate. They were both killed by the colossal blast, along with 1,175 other officers and men. The captain could not escape from the bridge when it was surrounded by a rising tide of flame from by far the most devastating and deafening explosion of the entire raid. Burning oil from the stricken battleship created a funeral pyre that dominated the sky over the harbor for many hours afterward. The ship canted over to port before settling on the bottom on an even keel, her shattered upperworks still showing. Only 337 members of her crew survived the worst single-ship disaster in American history.

Admiral Kidd and Captain Van Valkenburgh, whose bodies were never found, were each awarded the Medal of Honor. So was Lieutenant Commander Samuel Fuqua who, defying the encroaching inferno, helped one hundred injured sailors by directing their transfer by boat from the stern to the hospital ship USS *Solace*.

Arizona's commander, Captain Franklin Van Valkenburgh, had written to his wife on December 6, "By this time next week, we will be on our way home for Christmas." A day later, he and more than 1,100 others were dead.

(Above) A waterlogged service book salvaged from the USS *Arizona*. Its owner, Chief Machinist's Mate Andrew Jackson Bowen, Jr., was one of the 306 men who survived the battleship's destruction.

Many more sailors were plucked from the burning oil around the ship by small boats; others managed to swim to safety on Ford Island.

✪

ONBOARD THE NEIGHBORING *VESTAL*, COMMANDER CASSIN YOUNG, HER CAPTAIN, *proceeded to the bridge and later took personal command of the 3-inch antiaircraft gun. When blown overboard by the blast of the forward magazine explosion of the USS* Arizona, *to which the USS* Vestal *was moored, he swam back to his ship. The entire forward part of the USS* Arizona *was a blazing inferno with oil afire on the water between the two ships. As a result of several bomb hits, the USS* Vestal *was afire in several places, was settling and taking on a list. Despite severe enemy bombing and strafing at the time, and his shocking experience of having been blown overboard, Commander Young, with extreme coolness and calmness, moved his ship to an anchorage distant from the USS* Arizona *and subsequently beached the USS* Vestal *upon determining that such action was required to save the ship.*

— from Commander Young's Medal of Honor Citation

✪

The Navy Department regrets to inform you that your son, John Andrew Rauschkolb, Seaman First Class, US Navy, was lost in action in the performance of his duty and in the service of his country.

SO READ THE OFFICIAL TELEGRAM. MRS. RAUSCHKOLB, BACK HOME IN BELLEVILLE, ILLINOIS, was struck low by grief. The town paper ran the headline, "First Local Sailor Gives Life to US." A memorial service, attended by about three hundred people, was held in the town for the popular twenty-year-old signalman on the battleship *West Virginia*, sunk in harbor on December 7.

But Seaman Rauschkolb was not dead. In the chaos and confusion following the attack, scores of men were not traced for days, sometimes weeks, by the military bureaucracy, even though they were safe and well. They had often used their initiative to find somewhere else to make themselves useful. Rauschkolb dived beneath the burning oil on the surface of the water and managed to reach the battleship *Tennessee*, only lightly damaged. He joined impromptu firefighting teams in small boats, trying to tackle the flames on his own ship and, for a while, on the *Arizona*. The Navy Department did send a corrective telegram to his mother, but she never got over the shock and died in February 1942, one of many indirect victims of Pearl Harbor. Her son went home on compassionate leave to bury her.

The *West Virginia* fought hard and took a long time to go under, even after two 16-inch shell bombs penetrated deep into a hull already crippled by six torpedo hits. It was shrapnel from the bombs that mortally wounded Captain Mervyn Bennion. His gallant efforts to save his ship earned him the Medal of Honor. The man who tried to save him by lifting him bodily to a safer place, against the captain's orders, was a mess attendant, first

The huge explosion on the *Arizona* also damaged the repair ship *Vestal* (above), which was moored alongside. After sustaining several bomb hits that had been intended for nearby battleships, the *Vestal* was moved out of Battleship Row by her injured captain and beached after the attack to stop her from sinking. (Below) John Andrew Rauschkolb escaped the inferno on *West Virginia* by diving under a sea of burning oil and swimming to the lightly damaged *Tennessee*. In the post-battle confusion, Rauschkolb's mother was erroneously informed of his death — a shock from which she never recovered. (Overleaf) Forward and aft views of the burning *West Virginia*, resting upright on the harbor's shallow bottom.

"I stayed below until the flooding salt water and oil forced me to evacuate."

Eugene Merrill

Signalman B. Eugene Merrill had just stood down from his watch and was taking a shower when the first torpedo struck the USS *West Virginia*. He heard a muffled explosion, felt the ship shudder, and then the bow lift a few feet up before settling back down.

"What the hell was that?" one of the other men in the shower asked.

"Probably an explosion in the engine room," another replied.

Merrill tied a towel around his waist and headed aft toward his quarters. "I hadn't gone but a few steps when the second torpedo struck," he recalled. Almost immediately, General Quarters sounded over the loudspeaker.

"I headed for my battle station," Gene continued, "losing my towel, thongs, soap, and wash rag along the way." He arrived at the auxiliary signal station buck naked and joined one of the teams heading below to rescue the wounded. He lost count of the number of men he aided.

"When I emerged topside, the attack was over. The ship was sitting on the bottom with a port list, and burning." Merrill was one of the last men to leave.

class, named Doris Miller. One of the ship's stewards, he was also its heavyweight boxing champion and ran no risk of being mocked for his unusual given name. Miller showed his true mettle by taking over a machine gun as if born to the role, in the stricken battleship's notably fierce barrage of antiaircraft fire. Miller was the first black man to be awarded the Navy Cross.

Captain Mervyn Bennion

★

SEAMAN JOHN H. McGORAN WAS NINETEEN AND ACTING AS A signalman on the *California*, flagship of Vice Admiral William S. Pye, commanding the battleships of the Pacific Fleet. He was taking his breakfast dishes down to the scullery when the attack started. He joined the rush to battle stations, in his case one of the powder-handling rooms for the big guns. Once there, the men found the door locked; no one had the keys. Suddenly, the *California* lurched violently.

> A torpedo had hit us. The fuel tank next to our port magazine ignited in flames and there we were, surrounded on three sides by powder-filled magazines. We forced the lock on the magazine door and opened it. We discovered the covers had shaken off some of the cans containing the powder bags [for the 14-inch guns] and the aisle was strewn with ripped-open bags of gunpowder. Anxiously I entered, walking carefully over the debris to feel the bulkhead. I returned and reported to [Petty Officer First Class] Allen that the bulkhead was cool. Allen in turn passed the reassuring word over the mouthpiece of his headset to the bridge. . . .

> A bomb penetrated the decks above and exploded in front of the ship's store. It killed "Boots," one of the masters-at-arms [ship's policeman]. It bent a heavy steel hatch-coaming flush with the deck. We picked up our injured shipmate and carried him up to the first-aid station. As men brought in casualties, the Chief [petty officer from the engine room] would say, "Dead or alive? If they're dead, take them into the other room and throw them on the dead pile."

"above and beyond the call of duty"

DORIE MILLER
Received the Navy Cross
at Pearl Harbor, May 27, 1942

Mess Attendant Doris Miller (left) of the *West Virginia* risked his life to care for the battleship's mortally wounded skipper, Captain Mervyn Bennion (above, right), then manned a machine-gun post during the fierce attack. For his heroic efforts, he became the first black man to be awarded the Navy Cross (above). (Opposite) Still dressed in off-duty clothes, naval officers disembark from a launch as USS *California* burns in the background.

> *"A torpedo had hit us. The fuel tank next to our port magazine ignited in flames and there we were, surrounded on three sides by powder-filled magazines."*
>
> — John H. McGoran, Seaman on USS *California*

(Pages 114–115) Crewmen stream from the *California* as a flood of burning oil races toward her. *California*'s John McGoran (above) later aided in the rescue of sailors from the flaming waters. He can be seen in the color photograph of *West Virginia* and *Maryland* ablaze (right), standing on the left of the launch.

(Pages 116–117) The inferno of Battleship Row.

As I stood trying to comprehend all of this, someone handed me a bottle of root beer and a sandwich. Ordinarily I would have retched at the sight of so much blood, but I ate and drank, completely amazed at my appetite under such conditions and decided it was all incomprehensible. While I was in the first-aid station, word came to abandon ship.

Someone warned us that a wave of strafing Japanese planes was passing over. The planes came in low, firing their machine guns. Between sorties, men from nearby battle stations raced out on the quarterdeck and dragged to shelter those who had been struck by the machine-gun fire. Then, as soon as we felt it was safe, we ran for the motor launch, which was waiting for us at the port quarter. . . .

Only one who was there can fully appreciate what took place. As a Pearl Harbor survivor who was at ground-zero on Battleship Row [on] the morning of December 7, 1941, I feel, "if you didn't go through it, there's no words that can adequately describe it; if you were there, then no words are necessary."

No battleship present that day escaped unscathed. In the first wave of the attack, *Nevada* was hit by one torpedo while *Maryland* and *Tennessee* suffered minor damage and casualties. Amid such a record of destruction, it is usually forgotten that a tug and a drydock were also sunk — two unsung victims hit by the Japanese at Pearl Harbor along with nineteen warships.

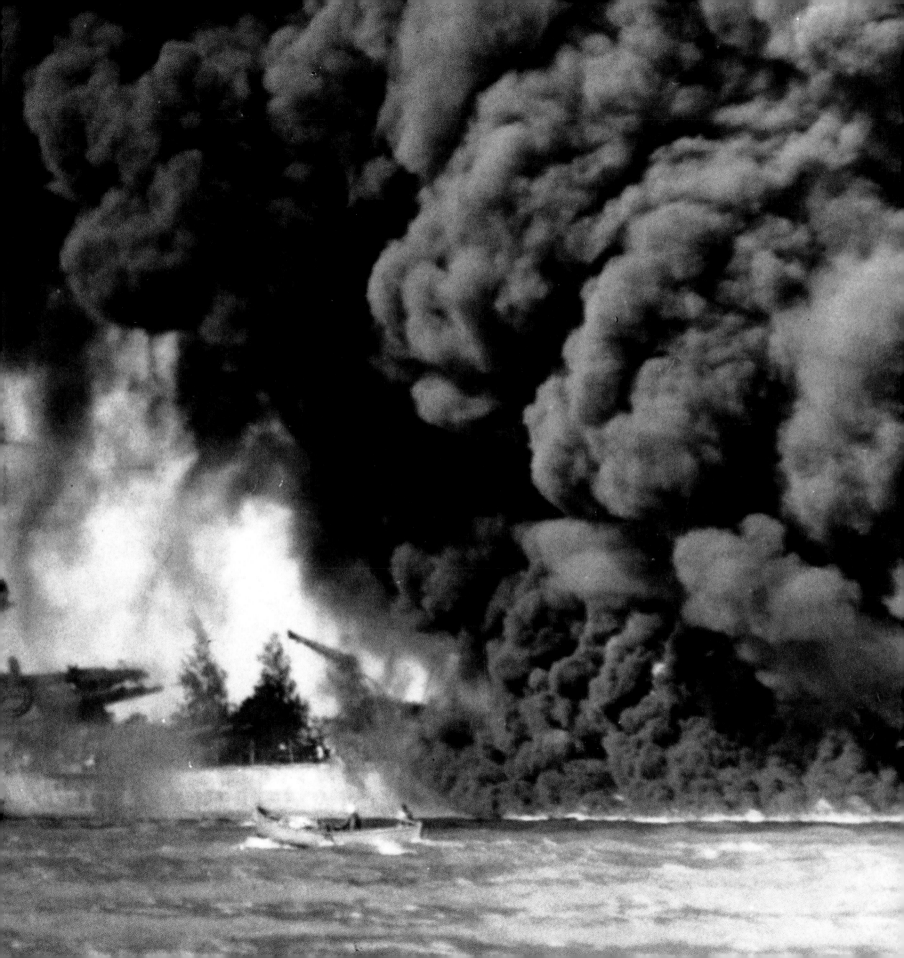

CHAPTER SEVEN | The Second Wave

"The mess hall was the natural place to take these [wounded] men. When we entered the mess hall, every single table had a man or a body stretched out on it."

— Air Maintenanceman Ted LeBaron

O BSERVING THE RUINATION OF HIS FLEET FROM HIS HEADQUARTERS IN THE LATER PHASES of the attack, Admiral Kimmel was hit lightly on the chest by a spent machine-gun bullet that came through a window. "It would have been merciful had it killed me," he told Commander Maurice Curts, the fleet communications officer standing next to him.

The obsessive Kimmel had left his wife behind in California and lived spartanly in a house not far from his headquarters, the better to concentrate on his huge responsibilities. He was just out of bed on the 7th when Commander Vincent Murphy, assistant war plans officer on duty at headquarters, phoned at 0740. He had news for the admiral of the attacks on submarines made by USS *Ward* and the PBY. The information had been mulled over by several staff officers, confirmed and reconfirmed with the units involved, checked, and rechecked. The admiral was awaiting yet more con- firmation on the attacks when Murphy called again.

Even as the two spoke, a signaller dashed into Murphy's office and shouted that Japanese planes were attacking, adding (inevitably) "This is no drill!" When the commander relayed the news, Kimmel hung up and dashed next door where the lawn afforded an unobstructed view of the harbor. The wife of Captain John Earle, chief of staff of the Fourteenth Naval District, was already standing there par- alyzed with shock as the enemy planes pirouetted over the base. For a few cataclysmic moments, the admiral watched the attack unfold in all its complexity — even witnessing the *Arizona* shift bodily with the impact of the bombs that rained down on it.

(Above) Bursts from exploding antiaircraft shells pepper a sky already filled with thick black smoke from burning ships. (Left) Armed with rifles and a machine gun, wary marines in a hastily dug foxhole await another attack by Japanese aircraft.

The protesting screech from the brakes of his official car shook Kimmel out of his own temporary paralysis. As he and his driver raced off to the admiral's office, another neighbor, Captain Freeland Daubin, commanding Submarine Squadron Four, made a flying leap onto the running board. They got to headquarters at 0805, the virtual height of the raid.

At 0812, Kimmel sent a signal to Admiral Stark, Chief of Naval Operations, in Washington: "Hostilities with Japan commenced with air raid on Pearl Harbor." He ordered his PBYs to "locate enemy force."

AT HIS QUARTERS AT FORT SHAFTER, A COUPLE OF MILES EAST OF PEARL HARBOR, GENERAL Short heard a series of explosions and came out onto his lanai to see what was going on. He had concluded that Navy or Marine pilots must be carrying out an unusually realistic practice when Colonel Walter Phillips, his chief of staff, came running at 0803 with the news that it was "the real thing" — a Japanese air attack. Short ordered the Army to Alert Number Three — preparation for an immediate invasion. Even so, the general could not believe it when told two battleships had sunk. "That's ridiculous!" he said, turning away from the bearer of bad news, Lieutenant Colonel George Bicknell, his deputy intelligence chief.

✪

THE FIRST WAVE LOST ONLY NINE PLANES to American gunners — five torpedo bombers, three fighters, and one dive-bomber. Fuchida's Kate had been hit by one or two American machine-gun bullets but none of the three men aboard was hurt and the attack commander continued to circle Oahu, carefully assessing the havoc being wrought by his men.

✪

THE "LULL" OF LESS THAN HALF AN HOUR between attack waves bore no resemblance to a rest period at ground level in Oahu. On Ford Island, the dispensary could not handle the hundreds of wounded men from the battleships. The mess hall, Marine barracks, and new bachelor-officers' quarters were pressed into service as dressing stations. Hundreds of volunteers as well as medical staff gave the injured blankets, first aid, food, drink, and comfort. Air maintenanceman Ted LeBaron remembered:

Thanks to the element of surprise, Japanese losses in the first wave were relatively light. (Above) This Zero, which crashed near Hickam Field, was one of just three fighters shot down as US Army servicemen scrambled to protect their base.

> *There had been many sailors who had either been blown into the water off the battleships or had jumped into the water to swim the short distance to Ford Island. The harbor was covered with oil from the torpedo hits and some drowned just trying to swim in the stuff. Some were wounded or burned before they entered the water. The mess hall was the natural place to take these men. When we entered the mess hall, every single table had a man or a body stretched out on it. The eerie thing about it was that you could have heard a pin drop.*

Aftermath in Honolulu

Although Honolulu was eight miles from Pearl Harbor, it was still close enough to suffer considerable damage from the fallout of the first attack and the second wave soon after. Only one Japanese bomb reportedly fell on the city, but spent Japanese bullets (left), as well as "friendly fire" in the form of fragments from American antiaircraft shells (below), and even the unexploded shells themselves falling back to earth, all had deadly consequences. As news of the attack by the Japanese spread throughout Honolulu, rumors began flying even faster than shrapnel. Frightened civilians, dealing with scanty information and the imposition of immediate curfews and blackouts, fueled stories of local Japanese uprisings and attacks by Fifth Columnist saboteurs.

(Above) Three American shipyard workers were killed when fragments of burst American antiaircraft shells peppered their car on the way to Pearl Harbor.
(Left) This Honolulu neighborhood was devastated by falling shells that burst into flames.
(Right) A Honolulu area schoolroom, its roof torn off, bears silent witness to the aftermath of the attack.

(Above) Naval gunners, holed up in an excavation for an uncompleted building at Kaneohe, scan the skies. (Opposite) A Kate, its bomb racks now empty, flies away from Kaneohe after the naval air station there was hit again in the second wave.

AS LOCAL RADIO SENT OUT CALLS TO SAILORS AND TROOPS TO RETURN TO THEIR UNITS, traffic chaos built up. At the same time, in scenes similar to those caused by the German *Blitzkrieg* in Europe in 1940, civilians were fleeing from Honolulu, blocking roads and compounding the pandemonium along the southern coast of Oahu. Honolulu itself was hit by just one Japanese bomb, but thirty-nine falling shells from American antiaircraft guns at Pearl Harbor eight miles away were understandably taken for enemy action. More radio appeals, this time to civilians to stay off the roads and indoors, were followed by a radio blackout that only intensified the general anxiety.

✪

DURING THE FIRST WAVE, HUNDREDS OF American sailors and soldiers, often acting without orders, had started shooting back, and were ready and waiting for the second assault. Everything from 5-inch ship's guns to regulation Colt .45 pistols and privately owned hunting rifles had been pressed into service. Chaplain Howell Forgy earned himself a memorable niche in history when he found a novel way of blessing the defensive efforts of sailors on the cruiser *New Orleans* as they manhandled shells in a power cut caused by a bomb blast at the Navy Yard. Amid the cacophony of explosions and the swelling roar of antiaircraft fire, he announced that there would be no church that morning. Handing out fruit to the human chain feeding the guns, he encouraged the men to "praise the Lord and pass the ammunition." The minister's mantra became an immensely popular song.

✪

IN THE GAP BETWEEN THE FIRST AND SECOND WAVES, MARINES AT EWA FIELD DISMOUNTED machine guns from crippled planes and were able to send up a hail of .50 caliber bullets when a group of Zeros from the second wave came over. But by 10 A.M. when Ewa was at last left alone, thirty-three of its planes, including eighteen dive-bombers and nine fighters, were destroyed or seriously damaged. Miraculously, only four men were killed and thirteen wounded in all this mayhem.

✪

LIEUTENANT COMMANDER SHIMAZAKI MUSTERED THE SECOND WAVE OF 167 AIRCRAFT TO strike one hour and one minute after the raid had begun. The first wave was still reassembling over Ewa at the southwestern extremity of Oahu when the second came in from due north, down the eastern side of the island. Thirty-five Zeros divided over the east coast

(Top) Sheet music for the song, "Praise The Lord And Pass The Ammunition," a popular hit in the weeks after Pearl Harbor and during the Pacific War. (Above) The song's title originated with Howell Forgy, Protestant chaplain aboard the cruiser USS *New Orleans*, who uttered the now-famous phrase amid the roar of battle.

"*We may then conclude
that anticipated results
have been achieved.*"

— Admiral Chuichi Nagumo, after hearing a report
on the *Akagi* from Commander Fuchida

"I remained with him until he died in my arms."

Armand "Pete" Pettricione

Just before the second attack wave, Seaman Second Class Pete Pettricione ran for cover with the rest of the men stranded on the tarmac at Kaneohe Naval Air Station. He and about twenty others made it to a nearby hangar and squeezed into a tiny room that could scarcely hold them all. Pete's friend and shipmate, John D. Buckley, was standing between him and the open door.

In minutes, the hangar was hit by two bombs and the strafing of machine guns which killed most of the men in the small, packed room. Pettricione and another of the few uninjured men began carrying the wounded and the dead out of the hangar.

"When I picked up [Seaman First Class Luther D.] Weaver to put his body on the truck, my hands went through his back."

Unfortunately, the base hospital was not equipped to deal with the flood of desperately wounded men, and many died for lack of medical attention. Pete's buddy, John Buckley, was still alive when he reached the hospital. He asked Pettricione to stay by his side.

"I remained with him until he died in my arms."

at Kahana Bay, seventeen swinging left to hit Kaneohe and Bellows Field while the rest went right to attack Ewa and Wheeler Field again. The fifty-four high-level bombers divided into three groups — nine to attack Ford Island, eighteen to attack Kaneohe, and twenty-seven to hit the HAF at Hickam. Eighty dive-bombers in four groups were detailed to attack Pearl Harbor.

Shimazaki gave the attack signal at 0854. He expected significant losses because he knew that his squadrons would be attacking an enemy awakened by his predecessors.

Ford Island was masked by the great pall of smoke caused by the first wave. The nine bombers assigned to it attacked the ships on the northwest side of the island instead. Light cruiser *Raleigh,* torpedoed in the first wave, was hit by a bomb aft. The *Detroit* in the next berth was straddled by bombs but unhit. Seaplane tender *Curtiss,* which was blazing away with her antiaircraft guns, took a direct hit from a bomb that exploded below deck and caused extensive damage. The ship was later hit by a shot-down Val, either by accident or

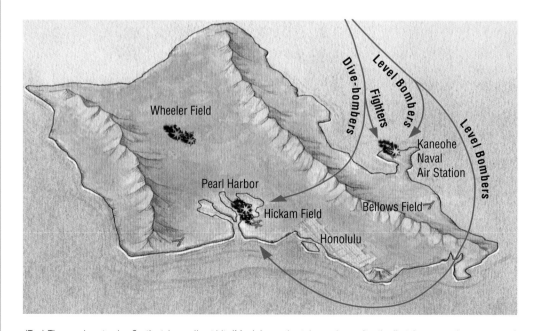

(Top) The seaplane tender *Curtiss* takes a direct hit. (Map) Approximately one hour after the first Japanese planes swooped down on Kaneohe and Pearl Harbor, the second wave unleashed its assault and also attacked Hickam and Wheeler Fields again. During this raid, the Army's Bellows Field, which had suffered only minor damage in the initial attack, was strafed by eight Zeros and five of its planes were quickly destroyed. Miraculously, only two men lost their lives.

on purpose, *kamikaze*-fashion. A dive-bomber ditched into the water a few hundred yards away and the pilot alone clambered onto the wing. He drew his pistol when a boat from a destroyer approached to pick him up and was promptly shot dead.

✪

THE MAIN ARMY FIELD AT HICKAM WAS RAIDED A SECOND TIME AT 0905, for eight minutes. Twenty-seven Kate high-level bombers renewed the onslaught on the parked planes and the many buildings on the base, while eighteen Zeros strafed. By this time, a soldier had mounted a machine gun in the nose of a bomber and only stopped shooting when forced to flee the fiery plane. Some antiaircraft guns blazed away after soldiers broke into locked ammunition stores. Other men manhandled machine guns, firing from the hip, or brandished small arms. An airman running along the line of burning hangars appeared to horrified witnesses to be running into the ground; his legs were being sliced away by a Zero. More men were killed as they tried to arm the exposed planes with guns, ammunition, and bombs. Four B-17s, twelve B-18s, and two A-20s were completely destroyed and many other other aircraft damaged. Of the HAF's total casualties — 174 killed, 336 wounded, and 43 missing — the vast majority fell at Hickam (145 dead, 274 injured, 27 unaccounted for).

Wheeler was subjected to a second attack by eight Zeros, lasting five minutes, that strafed more aircraft — some of which were on the move, trying to take off in order to confront the raiders. In all, eleven HAF pilots managed to get their planes into the air from Wheeler and Haleiwa (which was not attacked). They claimed eleven Japanese planes shot down. But eighty-three of Wheeler's planes, more than half, were destroyed or damaged on the ground. In the two attacks on the base, 27 Americans were killed, 53 wounded, and 6 not accounted for.

The Army's Bellows Field on the east coast, attacked by just one Zero of the first wave, was strafed by eight in the second, losing five planes, two men killed and four wounded. At unscathed Haleiwa, two Army pilots, Lieutenants Kenneth Taylor and George Welch, did their best for the honor of the HAF, despite having been up all night playing poker at Wheeler. From there, they phoned ahead to order fuel and ammunition for their P-40s before driving back to base in Taylor's car. Returning from a first flight for more fuel and ammunition, the pair took off again and joined the fray, shooting down four enemy planes. After another quick landing, they shot down three more, even though Taylor was hit in the arm. The pilots' contribution was one among many shining examples of a level of personal initiative that was so plentiful among junior officers and men that day — but so often woefully rare among the senior commanders.

During the second wave, some American fighters managed to take to the skies and engage in combat with the Japanese. Unfortunately, most of the fighter planes in Hawaii at the time were not of the first rank. Although the modern Curtiss P-40s (above and below) could hold their own, none of the many other fighters present on the American side at Pearl Harbor were a match for the speedy Japanese Zero.

"A couple of days later, I checked my plane in the hangar and counted some 450 holes."

Philip M. Rasmussen

At Wheeler, a pajama-clad Lieutenant Philip Rasmussen and a few fellow pilots worked frantically to arm and fuel their obsolescent P-36s. Finally, they managed to get them aloft between attacks. Once airborne, they received word that Kaneohe was under attack again.

"At 9000 feet, we spotted dive-bombers and dove to attack them."

Rasmussen "stitched" one Japanese plane with machine-gun fire, then pulled up, dodging another Japanese pilot intent on ramming him. Then a Japanese fighter found him.

"At that instant, all hell broke loose. My canopy was shot off. I felt the plane shudder [as I] lost control and tumbled into the clouds below."

The plane's hydraulic control lines had been severed, the tail wheel shot off, and "two 20mm cannon shells had buried themselves in the radio behind the pilot's seat."

The radio had saved Rasmussen's life. Somehow, he managed to regain control of his aircraft. Without rudder, brakes, or tail wheel, he made it back to Wheeler and landed safely.

"I shakily got out of my plane, walked over to my room and traded my pajamas for a flying suit, then returned to the flight line."

IN THE HARBOR OF HONOLULU, THE NEWLY COMBATANT UNITED States acquired its first active allies: the Dutch seamen of the SS *Jagersfontein*, which arrived from the Netherlands East Indies at 0900 and promptly opened fire with her antiaircraft guns.

AMID THE WELTER OF INDIVIDUAL ATTACKS MADE BY THE SECOND wave, a bomb hit the jetty next to the light cruiser *Honolulu*, which was significantly damaged by the blast. Her already battered sister *Helena* was rocked but not further damaged by several near misses. A quarter of a mile to the south, the fleet flagship *Pennsylvania*, twin of the *Arizona*, was hit by a single bomb in her dry dock. Two dozen men were killed and thirty-eight wounded. The second wave also accounted for the destroyers *Cassin* and *Downes*, marooned side by side in dock immediately ahead of the *Pennsylvania*. In the adjacent floating dry dock, the destroyer *Shaw* was shattered by the three bombs that bored into her innards. The explosion at about 1000, when her forward magazine went up, breaking her back, was exceeded only by the blast that killed the *Arizona*.

(Right) Near the end of the second wave, three bombs hit the American destroyer *Shaw* in dry dock, setting off her magazines in a spectacular explosion.
(Left) USS *Shaw*'s bell, now housed at the United States Naval Academy's museum.

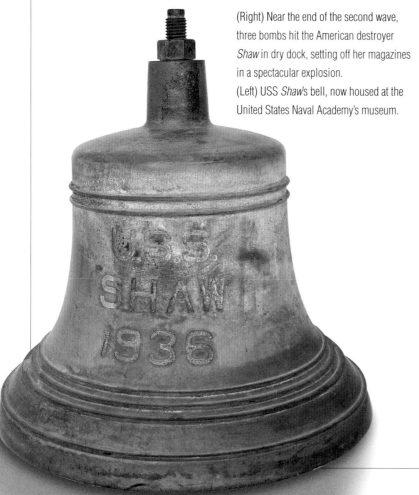

REAR ADMIRAL FURLONG'S COMMAND IN THE FIRST MINUTES OF THE BATTLE, "ALL SHIPS sortie," was not the easiest to carry out in the heat of a sneak attack. But during the lull, various ships began pulling away from their moorings, making for the relative safety of the open sea — and perhaps a chance to confront their attackers. In the hurry to get away, many went minus their full crews. On the destroyer *Blue*, the only officers aboard that Sunday morning were four young ensigns, who cast off at 0847, their commander in hot pursuit behind them in a ship's boat.

The *Nevada* was the only battleship to make a run for the open sea. Although damaged by a single torpedo that tore a house-sized hole in her port bow during the first wave, she managed to get up steam in forty-five minutes and headed for the channel. As senior officer present, Lieutenant Commander J.F. Thomas was in charge on the bridge as Lieutenant Lawrence Ruff and Quartermaster Robert Sedberry steered the battered ship past the blazing *Arizona* — three of whose sailors managed to clamber aboard and volunteered to man a machine gun.

The dive-bombers of the second wave saw her moving and twenty-three attacked, hoping to sink her and block the channel, shutting down the harbor. At least five scored direct hits, starting fires and holing the hull twice underwater. Luckily, the main magazines were empty, as the ship was awaiting a delivery at the time of the attack. Seaman Earl R. Lester's battle station was at an ammunition hoist beneath a 5-inch gun on the main deck aft:

She was listing badly forward. When the second attack came, we started putting shells in the hoist on the double again, and there was a great blast that nearly knocked me over. I was so scared I didn't know what, but we stayed there until the hoist was out of operation. We stood by to help out with the wounded. Some had legs gone; others were blind and hurt so bad you couldn't help them. They were cut so badly from shrapnel, they were just covered with blood.

[She] was listing so bad we had to beach her. Some tugs pushed us on the beach.

Realizing that their ship was not going to make the open sea and determined not to block the channel, the trio at the helm ran her aground at Hospital Point on the eastern side of the channel entrance. For his gallantry during the ordeal, Machinist Donald K. Ross was awarded the Medal of Honor. So was Chief Boatswain Edwin J. Hill — posthumously.

✪

ONE OTHER OF THE HANDFUL OF SHIPS THAT MANAGED TO GET UNDER WAY FROM HER mooring (in the Southeast loch eastward of the dock area) was the light cruiser *St. Louis*, at 0930. The accelerating ship headed due south down the channel to the exit. As she emerged, lookouts on the starboard side were horrified to see two torpedo tracks in the water, coming from ahead at an angle of forty-five degrees. There was nothing to be done and the men on the bridge froze like rabbits caught in a headlight, bracing them-

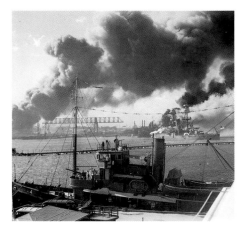

Between attacks, the battleship *Nevada* managed to raise steam and get underway. During the second wave, she was pummeled by Japanese dive-bombers that hoped to sink her in the harbor mouth and bottle up the American fleet. (Top) Badly hit, *Nevada* prepares to run aground. (Above) Caught by the current, the battleship begins to swing around. (Below) The damage from a bomb hit to her bow. (Right) Finally, with the aid of fleet tugs, *Nevada* ran aground on the western side of the harbor entrance.

Yamamoto's Secret Weapon

The most closely guarded secret of the whole Pearl Harbor operation involved the use of midget submarines. Admiral Yamamoto had included them in his plans with extreme reluctance and only at the strong insistence of his submariners. Yet these ill-fated weapons reveal much about Japanese military thinking.

In underlying concept, these pint-size, two-man, two-torpedo submersibles were "human-piloted torpedoes," to quote one Japanese theorist of the 1930s. Since the midget subs had a maximum range of less than a hundred miles when surfaced and considerably less when submerged, the Pearl Harbor plan all but sealed the fates of their crews. (None reached the designated pick-up point and only one man, Sakamaki, survived.) But to Japanese naval tacticians, their smallness and speed promised an irresistible combination of stealth and surprise.

Originally, the midget submarines were intended to be battleship killers in a pivotal high-seas contest between the American and Japanese fleets. Launched from their mother ship, a former seaplane tender lagging well behind the main fleet, they would wait until the haze of battle provided camouflage, then streak to attack the enemy's capital ships. Such a stratagem grew logically from Japan's long-held belief that the key to success against the United States Navy was to engineer a quick and decisive defeat over a superior force.

As it turned out, the midgets never played their intended role in a conventional sea battle. Their most significant actions after Pearl were attacks on the harbors of Sydney, Australia, and Diego Suarez in Madagascar. And on December 7, 1941, the midgets came perilously

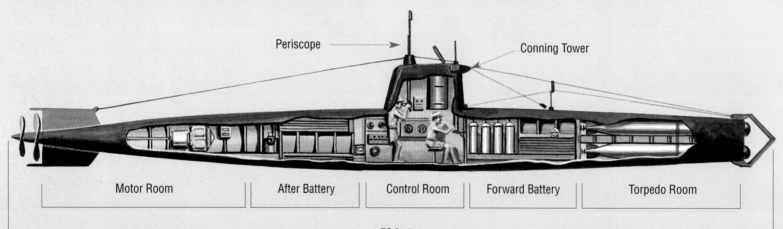

Periscope — Conning Tower

| Motor Room | After Battery | Control Room | Forward Battery | Torpedo Room |

78 feet

(Above) This cutaway shows the midget submarine's cramped interior. (Right) Sakamaki's submarine, washed ashore near Bellows Field. (Left) The midget sub spotted by *Monaghan* was later raised from the sea floor at Pearl Harbor. Rammed by *Monaghan*, she was also hit by a shell from *Curtiss*. The washboard effect on the sub's hull was caused by the concussion from *Monaghan's* depth charges.

selves for the shock. But the 18-inch torpedoes buried themselves in a small coral reef off the entrance and exploded harmlessly. Then the lookouts spotted the conning tower of a midget submarine 1,000 yards to the southwest, and several salvos were fired by the four 5-inch secondary guns on the starboard side. The submarine disappeared.

✪

THUS AS IT BEGAN, SO IT ENDED — WITH A US WARSHIP FIRING on a Japanese submarine off the mouth of Pearl Harbor. For the controversial midgets, Pearl Harbor had not been a good day. After their run-ins with the destroyer *Ward* and the PBY early that morning, another had been spotted within Pearl Harbor during the attack, only to be fired upon, then rammed and depth-charged by the destroyer *Monaghan*. Another simply disappeared. The fifth was poor Ensign Sakamaki's, which proved uncontrollable without its gyrocompass. It pitched and yawed, jerked up and down, failed to get into the harbor, was depth-charged at least once, ran out of battery power, drifted, and finally grounded itself on a coral reef. To make sure the little sub didn't fall into American hands, Sakamaki lit the fuse for its explosive charges, then he and his crewman, Petty Officer Inagaki, lept overboard. He lost Inagaki in the heavy surf (the body washed up later), then realized to his horror that the charges had not ignited. He tried to swim back, but his strength failed him. He gave up and let the sea take him. When he came to, he was sprawled on a beach. Probably the first sight he saw were the heavy boots and canvas gaiters of the American soldier standing guard over him. Sakamaki was the first Japanese soldier or sailor to be made a prisoner of war by the United States.

His little sub was salvaged and subsequently put on show during bond drives. Some experts believe that the midgets scored at least one torpedo hit. But that can hardly be seen as a triumph, especially when compared with the achievement of Fuchida's seven hundred airmen who had so vehemently opposed their inclusion in the attack plan. In the Japanese propaganda photograph commemorating the undoubted bravery of the submariners, Sakamaki was carefully airbrushed out. Under the *bushido* code of the samurai, surrender and capture were totally dishonorable and grounds for suicide, with no option. In the eyes of Japanese militarists, his chief crime was staying alive afterward.

Ensign Kazuo Sakamaki

Ensign Sakamaki's sword (left), which he carried with him aboard his midget submarine, was later taken away by his American captors. (Below) A surprisingly cheerful Sakamaki poses for his POW photograph. The fact that Sakamaki was captured alive by the Americans made him a disgrace in his country's eyes. In a subsequent propaganda portrait honoring the Pearl Harbor submariners (bottom), he is conspicuously absent.

KAZUO SAKAMAKI ISN HJ 1 MI

KAZUO SAKAMAKI ISN HJ 1 MI

Part Three **AFTERMATH**

CHAPTER EIGHT

The Price of Admiralty

THE LAST ATTACKER FLEW AWAY AT 0945. LAST OF ALL TO LEAVE WAS COMMANDER Fuchida's lightly damaged Kate. All surviving planes landed back on their carriers, then about 190 miles north of Oahu, between 1030 and 1330. One straggler and Fuchida were the last to touch down. The second wave had suffered significantly more damage than the first. Twenty planes (12.4 percent) were shot down, bringing the total destroyed in the entire attack to twenty-nine (8.3 percent, specifically nine Zeros, fifteen Vals, five torpedo Kates). And fifty-five Japanese airmen were killed. This ratio of about eight percent of fatalities in an extremely daring and complicated attack against a well-armed enemy was well within the margin of military "acceptability."

(Left) One of the last attacking Kate bombers heads back to the carriers as thick smoke below bears witness to the destruction at Hickam Field (at far left), the dry docks at Pearl Harbor (at middle) and Battleship Row (at right). (Above) A Kate prepares to land on *Akagi*'s deck. (Pages 134–135) USS *Enterprise* passes a still-burning *Arizona* as she returns to harbor at dusk on December 8.

The overwhelming majority of losses were, of course, on the American side — thanks largely to the factor of surprise so ruthlessly exploited by a well-trained enemy. The US Navy was permanently or temporarily deprived of some 300,000 tons of shipping — including nineteen warships. In all, 2,390 Americans died on December 7, 1941, or from their wounds shortly afterward, and 1,178 were injured. The Navy lost 1,999 killed and 710 wounded; the Marines 109 and 69; the Army 233 and 364. Forty-nine civilians were also killed and thirty-five wounded. Fifteen men, all from the Navy, were awarded the nation's highest decoration, the Congressional Medal of Honor — most of them posthumously. Fifty-one Navy Crosses and three US Navy and Marine Corps medals were awarded. Five Army men won the Distinguished Service Cross and sixty-five soldiers and four sailors were decorated with the Silver Star. The unusual honor of being received by Emperor Hirohito was bestowed on Genda and Fuchida.

(Above) As a returning Kate approaches *Akagi*, the crews stand ready. The small white posts stretch the aircraft carrier's arrestor cables across the deck. (Right) A Zero fighter touches down in front of *Akagi*'s island.

AN ELATED COMMANDER GENDA AND AN EXHAUSTED FUCHIDA HAD tried to persuade their admiral to launch a second attack on the way home. Yamamoto left the decision to "nervous Nagumo" as the man in the best place to judge. But the Combined Fleet supremo knew full well which way his task force commander would jump, before the signal that the carriers were returning reached the Japanese fleet flagship, *Nagato,* in home waters. Overruling the impassioned pleas of the airmen, who wanted to follow the ancient military principle of exploiting a victory to the limit, Nagumo set a westerly course for Japan.

Thus the two tank farms, with 4,500,000 barrels of fuel oil, and the indispensable ship-repair facilities at Pearl Harbor — the pre-determined objectives of a second attack — remained untouched. The US Navy did not need to retreat 2,200 miles to the West Coast. Yet Fuchida's airmen had achieved Yamamoto's stated objective by sidelining for half a year the only force that might have blocked Japan's southward expansion. Nagumo therefore felt entitled to say, "Mission accomplished." The great leap southward succeeded beyond the junta's rashest forecasts. In five months, against a fragmented Allied opposition, Japan conquered a great swath of territory and islands, including British Malaya and Singapore, the Dutch East Indies, and finally the Philippines. The Greater East Asia Co-Prosperity Sphere was complete, and Japan now had access to all the land and raw materials it could use.

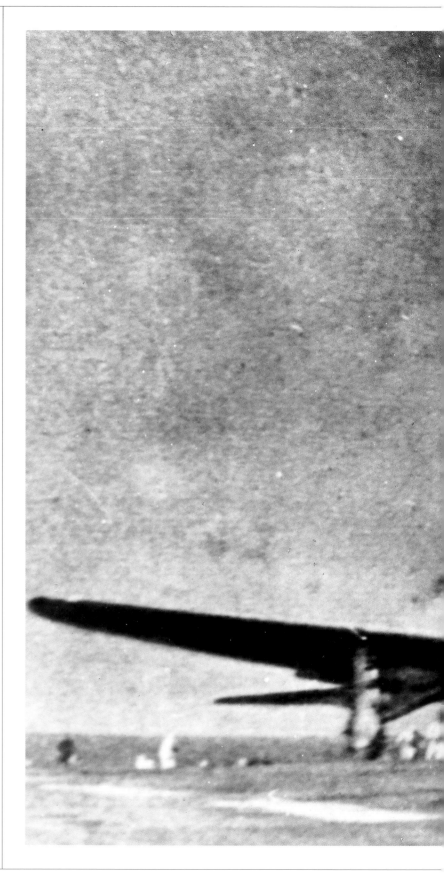

Japan Conquers an Empire

After Pearl Harbor, the Japanese moved quickly to occupy an empire in the Western Pacific before the United States could respond. They took Guam and Wake, and landed in the Philippines. In mid-February 1942, the vaunted British stronghold of Singapore and its nearly 140,000 service personnel surrendered, paving the road to the Dutch East Indies and its precious supplies of oil. By March, Japan had seized control of all the Southeast Asian and West Pacific possessions of France, Britain, and the Netherlands, and it also now controlled most of the Philippines. This ensured the supplies of raw materials it would need. If the conquerors had now paused to consolidate their gains, the Pacific War could well have lasted much longer. Instead, they pressed onward, suffering a devastating defeat at the Battle of Midway in June. Though the Japanese would extend their reach as far as the Eastern Solomons, they would never win a major battle against the Americans. When US marines landed on Guadalcanal in August 1942, they halted the Japanese advance and irrevocably turned the tide of war.

In the wake of Pearl Harbor, the Japanese rolled across Southeast Asia. Their armies swept down through Malaya, capturing Singapore on February 15, 1942 (opposite, top), and poured ashore in the Dutch East Indies (top). (Above) The British cruiser, HMS *Exeter*, sinks on March 1, 1942, one of several Allied casualties of the disastrous battle of the Java Sea and its aftermath. (Bottom left) American troops in the Philippines retreated into the tunnels of Corregidor Island, along with their commander, Douglas MacArthur (bottom right, in cap). On May 6, 1942, Corregidor surrendered to the Japanese (right).

Occupation on Niihau

After Pearl Harbor was hit, the people of the small Hawaiian island of Niihau found themselves under Japanese occupation — by a pilot whose damaged plane crashed there while returning to its carrier. Benehakka Kanahele (above) and his wife Ella (top) were taken prisoner, but Kanahele succeeded in overcoming and killing their captor.

THE REMOTE ISLAND OF NIIHAU WAS THE ONLY OTHER PART OF THE TERRITORY OF HAWAII affected by the strike on Pearl Harbor. Well to the west of Oahu and the last stop before Midway, its only link with the outside world was the Monday sampan from the next island a few miles to the east, Kauai. The peace was brutally disturbed at about 2 P.M. on December 7, 1941, when Pilot Shigenori Nishikaichi flew over in his shot-up, sputtering Zero and crash-landed in a field. Local resident Hawila Kaleohano struggled successfully with the trapped flier for his pistol and even seized his papers when locals took the pilot prisoner.

A thirty-year-old ethnic Japanese islander named Harada was recruited to act as interpreter. It was from their prisoner that the people of Niihau first learned of the air attack on Oahu. Because of the resulting chaos after the attack, the weekly sampan did not arrive and, after a few days, Harada threw in his lot with the pilot. He stole a shotgun and a pistol, and took control as the local people hid in the fields. The Japanese pair dismounted the Zero's machine guns and recovered the pilot's pistol from Mr. Kaleohano's house, which they torched. But Benehakka Kanahele and another islander managed to steal the ammunition for the guns while six men sneaked away in a boat and rowed all night to Kauai. They brought back Aylmer Robinson, Niihau's main landowner, and a detachment of troops in a tender.

But by the time help arrived, the "occupation" was over. Kanahele and his wife Ella had tried to ambush the two Japanese but were taken prisoner. The couple bravely made a grab for the guns pointed at them and a four-cornered melee developed, during which Kanahele was shot twice. Totally enraged, the big islander picked up the pilot bodily and smashed his head against a wall, killing him. Harada then let go of Mrs. Kanahele, snatched up the shotgun, and killed himself. Kaleohano and a fully recovered Kanahele were later decorated for their bravery.

✪

AN EMOTION NOT SO DIFFERENT FROM MR. KANAHELE'S SWEPT ACROSS THE UNITED STATES as Americans absorbed the shock of the attack on Pearl Harbor. Millions gathered around radios to hear how the President captured the public mood with his appeal to a joint session of Congress the next day. At 12:29 P.M. Washington time, Roosevelt asked the legislature to exercise its constitutional prerogative and declare war on Japan:

> *Yesterday, December 7, 1941 — a date which will live in infamy — the United States of America was suddenly and deliberately attacked by naval and air forces of the Empire of Japan. . . .*
>
> *As commander in chief of the Army and Navy, I have directed that all measures be taken for our defense.*
>
> *Always will we remember the character of the onslaught against us. . . . I ask that the Congress declare that since the unprovoked and dastardly attack by Japan on Sunday, December 7, a state of war has existed between the United States and the Japanese Empire.*

The Senate said "aye" by 82 votes to none; the House of Representatives followed suit by 388 votes to 1. The nation united in its will to wage the war that Roosevelt had long since identified as inevitable. Young Americans in the thousands rushed to volunteer. In beleaguered London, Churchill rejoiced, especially when Hitler and Mussolini declared war on the United States. America was now fully engaged in the worldwide conflict.

✪

KIMMEL'S ORDER TO FIND THE JAPANESE carriers was obeyed, but the response was too little, too late. That night, Admiral Halsey's *Enterprise* task force sent planes toward the Japanese Marshall Islands southwest of Hawaii, launching twenty-eight in all. Six were F4F fighters, which were ordered to land at Ford Island to refuel. Despite repeated warnings that they were coming, nervous gunners on the *Pennsylvania* and all over the harbor opened fire, downing four and killing three American pilots.

Rumors abounded on Oahu as trigger-happy sailors and troops opened fire on each other, on shadows, on unexpected vehicles or on purported invaders who were reported to be landing in droves, by parachute as well as by boat. The blackout imposed from the evening of December 7 did not help. At the behest of General Short, Territorial Governor Joseph B. Poindexter declared martial law throughout Hawaii on the afternoon of December 7, a move without precedent in American history. The next day, HAF pilots shot up four fishing boats off Barbers Point, killing six

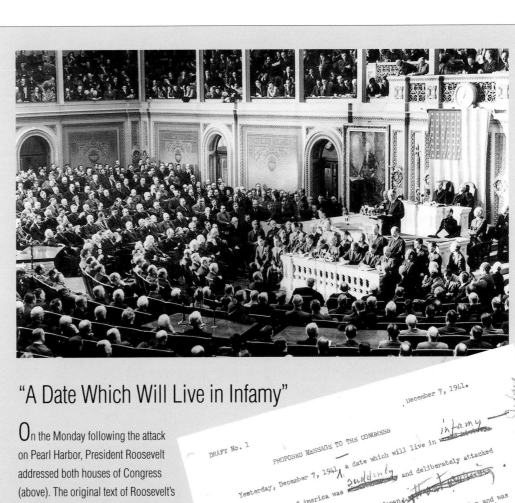

"A Date Which Will Live in Infamy"

On the Monday following the attack on Pearl Harbor, President Roosevelt addressed both houses of Congress (above). The original text of Roosevelt's speech (right), bearing his own corrections. The now-famous phrase Roosevelt wrote was, "A date which will live in infamy," not as is more commonly quoted, "a day." (Below) Wearing a black mourning band on his sleeve, President Roosevelt signs the declaration of war.

> "...we were all so busy and in such a state of shock, we didn't have time to be afraid."

Celeste Pilvelis and Albert Brauer

When Second Lieutenant Celeste Pilvelis began her duty shift at the Army's Tripler General Hospital early on the morning of Sunday, December 7, she was still basking in the romantic glow of the previous evening — spent with her handsome young fiancé at the new Officers' Club at Hickam Air Force Base. First Lieutenant Albert Brauer was stationed with the Nineteenth Infantry at Schofield Barracks. As soon as Celeste finished her shift, Albert had promised to take her to the beach for the afternoon.

Albert Brauer, meanwhile, was in his barracks when he heard explosions outside his window. "My God, the general's calling maneuvers on Sunday,'" he thought in dismay. The last thing he wanted to do was cancel his plans with Celeste.

Then he noticed ambulances heading across Wheeler Field, located next to the barracks. As news of the raid quickly spread, everyone jumped into action. Brauer and a number of other men made their way to the roof of the barracks, where several machine-gun stands had already been set up.

"All the ammunition was locked up," he said. "I don't know how they got it."

At the hospital, which was on the northwest edge of Honolulu, Celeste found herself dealing with an unbelievable stream of casualties — all arriving at the same time.

"There were men with arms and legs blown off."

As she and the medical staff struggled to cope with the horror of the attack's aftermath, Celeste scanned the faces of each new group of wounded and dying — and prayed that Albert would not be among them. For the next four days, she stayed at the hospital and worked around the clock. There was no time — and, in fact, no way — to find out if her fiancé was alive or dead. It was almost a week before Celeste knew that Albert was safe. In the meantime, both her parents, and Albert's, were anxious for news of their children.

"I was finally able to send a telegram to my parents, after four or five days, to let them know I was all right. Albert couldn't get through to his parents, so I managed to send a telegram for him to his mother."

In the days following the attack, "we had to paint the windows black before we were allowed to have any lights turned on in the hospital," Celeste remembered. "But we were all so busy and in such a state of shock, we didn't have time to be afraid."

Celeste and Albert were married in a chapel at Fort Shafter, on Oahu, in June 1942, and both survived the war. Albert remained in military service for twenty-four years — including five years at Schofield — and retired with the rank of lieutenant colonel.

(Above, left) Albert Brauer and Celeste Pilvelis, shortly after they fell in love in prewar Oahu. (Right) A formal portrait of First Lieutenant Albert Brauer, taken at Schofield's photography studio. (Above right) One of Albert's favorite snaps of Celeste. (Top) The telegram Celeste sent to Albert's parents five days after the attack.

"...the strange became normal after a while...."

Muriel Williams

On the morning of December 7, Muriel Williams was getting her eldest son ready for Sunday school. She and her husband, a boatswain's mate first class, lived in the Navy housing units close by the Navy Yard at Pearl Harbor. Clifford Williams had recently transferred to the Navy Yard after serving for almost four years on the USS *Arizona*. Duty called, even on Sunday, and he had already left for work.

As Muriel was helping her son get dressed, she was interrupted by shouting from the neighboring second-floor balcony:

"Muriel, you'd better get up! The Japs are bombing the hell out of the Navy Yard!"

Scarcely believing what she had just heard, Muriel raced outside. The acrid smell of black smoke from the destruction on Battleship Row was already filling the air. Overhead, she could clearly make out the Japanese planes.

"They were flying at tree level and one pilot was so close that I could see the white headband he wore."

Muriel ran back into the house. Within minutes, orders came for all families at the Navy quarters to stay indoors until evacuation later that afternoon. But there was no news about Clifford or any of the other men at the Navy Yard.

That night — and in the midst of a curfew and blackout — Muriel and her two young sons stayed with friends in Honolulu. They returned home two days later, to the happy news that Clifford had survived unharmed.

"It was only after a few days that it hit us as to what could have happened and then I became fearful for my family," Muriel recalled.

For the next few weeks, the young Navy wife hardly saw her husband. Whenever Clifford managed to get home, it was only to change his clothes. With a curfew and blackout still in effect, Muriel and the boys rarely left the house. And if they did venture out at all, they took along gas masks.

"It was odd how the strange became normal after a while and we adjusted to the conditions. I cleaned house even though I wasn't sure how long I would be staying, and my neighbor baked cookies."

Muriel and Clifford had many close friends among the crew of the *Arizona* and had spent the evening of Saturday, December 6, with the ship's bandleader, Fred Kinney.

(Left) Muriel and Clifford Williams in 1947, shortly after Clifford was transferred back to Pearl Harbor. (Below) Their spartan unit at the Navy housing quarters was second from the right. (Top) Because of heightened security and blackouts immediately after the attack, Muriel used this official card to communicate with her family.

"Fred was a dear friend, and wherever he and the band were, so were we."

The entire band perished when the *Arizona* blew up. When Muriel visited the *Arizona* Memorial years later and stood reading the names of so many of her husband's former shipmates, she realized, "The faces of the friends I was recalling were young — time stopped for them on December 7, 1941, and they will be forever young through all eternity."

Muriel and her sons left for the safety of the mainland in June of 1942. It was almost a year before the family was reunited. Muriel and Clifford celebrated their fiftieth wedding anniversary in 1985, shortly before he passed away.

EYEWITNESS

"[The planes] were flying so low I could clearly see their markings."

James Shigeru Wada

As usual on a Sunday morning, thirteen-year-old James Wada was caddying at the Waialae Golf Course east of Waikiki. Sunday was the only day James didn't help work his family's small farm. His parents, who were Japanese immigrants to Hawaii, raised hogs as well as some chickens and a few ducks.

The golfers were just approaching the ninth green when the first wave of airplanes heading for Pearl Harbor appeared. "I knew immediately they were Japanese," Wada remembered. "They were flying so low I could clearly see their markings." His employer, however, didn't seem to notice. The men finished playing the ninth hole and started toward the tenth tee. Wada was relieved: "The guy I was caddying for was a regular. He was a good tipper."

They reached the tenth tee just as the second wave stormed overhead. People started streaming out of the nearby clubhouse, shouting, "We're at war!" As far as James was concerned, the "we" included him, too. "For us, there was no question," he would later say. "We were Americans."

fishermen. Many other people on Oahu were wounded or frightened out of their wits by "friendly fire."

The strongest rumors on Oahu immediately after the raid concerned an alleged "fifth column" among the ethnic Japanese population. Japanese laborers had "cut arrows in crops pointing toward Pearl Harbor"; Japanese saboteurs had "poisoned the water supply"; a Japanese spy "sent signals by a blue lamp" from behind Fort Shafter — all myths, but also symptomatic of tension between ethnic Japanese and the rest of the population. Many on Oahu and all over America believed the Japanese incapable of such a strike unaided, and thought the Germans were behind it. A heavy police guard protected the consulate general in Honolulu from public wrath. The building, however, was thoroughly searched by detectives. Tens of thousands of Japanese and Japanese Americans (*Nisei*) would soon be interned in camps in the western states for the duration of the war — a dark episode for which the US government apologized half a century later.

✪

KIMMEL AND SHORT WERE RELIEVED of their commands on December 17, pending a full investigation of the disaster. Revisionist historians have described them as "scapegoats." But a scapegoat, as commonly understood, is the *innocent* bearer of transferred guilt. The sole duty of the two commanders was jointly to protect America's principal outpost against attack, whether or not they thought, or were even misled by Washington into thinking, that the blow

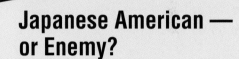

Japanese American — or Enemy?

In the panicky days after Pearl Harbor, many people feared that Japanese soldiers might soon be wading ashore on American beaches. Fanned by the press, public pressure quickly grew for the government to do something about what many people viewed as a potential "fifth column" — the Japanese Americans living on the Pacific coast. Although many of these were native-born Americans with few ties to Japan, some 110,000 Japanese Americans in California, Washington, and Oregon were moved inland to bleak internment camps during the spring and summer of 1942. All their assets were seized and sold.

People of Japanese ethnic origin in Hawaii — the largest minority in the islands' prewar ethnic quilt — also fell victim to the growing public fear of a Japanese invasion. After the attack, their cameras and radios were taken away, language schools closed, and newspapers censored. But there was no large-scale attempt to intern the 150,000 residents of Japanese heritage; to have done so would have brought the islands to a virtual standstill. Hawaii's Japanese Americans subsequently proved their loyalty to the United States, and many served with distinction in the Armed Forces.

Life on Oahu took on a surreal quality following the attack. (Above) Swimmers walk by barbed wire on the beach at Waikiki. (Left) Wary civil defense workers man a makeshift bunker piled high with sandbags. (Right, top) Civilians line up for food at a grocery store, its windows taped as a precaution against the concussion from bomb blasts. (Right, bottom) A soldier stands guard outside a Honolulu radio station.

George DeLong

Seaman George DeLong was just crawling out of his bunk in the bowels of the USS *Oklahoma* when the attack began.

"All of a sudden, we heard the loudspeaker system turn on and the boatswain's mate hollered, 'All hands man your battle stations!'"

Watertight doors started slamming shut. Before DeLong or any of the other men in his section could react, there was an explosion, quickly followed by two more.

DeLong recalled that the ship started to turn over almost immediately. Trapped, he and his companions frantically stuffed mattresses and a convenient game board into a ventilator spewing water into their compartment. From somewhere, they found a twenty-five-pound wrench.

"Two of us had been to quartermaster school, so we knew Morse Code and thought: 'We'll just start banging on the bulkhead.'" For hours, as the water slowly rose and the air grew stale, DeLong and his shipmates took turns hammering out S-O-S.

Finally, someone answered. Overhead on the upturned hull, rescue crews were frantically cutting through the capsized *Oklahoma* with compression drills.

Soon, DeLong sucked in fresh sea air, his first in over thirty hours.

"I don't know why I remember, but I was the fifth one out."

would fall somewhere else. They failed to defend. They failed to coordinate, before and during the attack.

The mountains of evidence from eight investigations do not even support the compromise proposition that they were "as much sinned against as sinning." While Washington was obviously guilty of contributory negligence, Kimmel and Short had to pay the price for comprehensive defeat — the other side of the coin of high rank.

Yet the fair-minded observer cannot avoid pitying the two leaders, denied any further role in the war or their day in court, their lives ruined amid endless self-justifications to which fewer and fewer would listen. Like any protagonist in an ancient Greek tragedy, they were brought low by their own failings.

Kimmel, who realistically tore two of the four stars off his uniform immediately after the attack, duly went back to his substantive rank of rear admiral. Rear Admiral Chester W. Nimitz made a double leap in the opposite direction to replace him as CINCPAC, perhaps the most inspired American appointment of World War II.

✪

A VAST SALVAGE OPERATION BEGAN EVEN as the last raiders were flying back to their carriers. One man emerged from the *Utah* when rescuers cut into the hull. Six more were saved by similar methods from the upturned *Oklahoma*. As work continued on December 8, two more groups of eleven and thirteen men respectively were cut free — a total of thirty-two were extricated from the hulk. But it was only in June 1942, after the raised *West Virginia* was towed into

(Above) The *West Virginia*, raised from the bottom after the attack, sets sail for a mainland dockyard.

dry dock, that twenty bodies were found inside her. Scratches on a bulkhead revealed that at least some of the men were still alive on December 23.

Captain Homer Wallin's Pearl Harbor Salvage Organization, formally set up on January 9, 1942, was a remarkable demonstration of the American "can do" spirit that would become such a feature of the US advance across the Pacific.

The beached *Nevada* and the sunken *West Virginia* and *California* rejoined the colors, as did the less badly damaged *Tennessee, Maryland,* and *Pennsylvania*. (The latter five, together with the USS *Mississippi*, had the distinction of winning the Battle of the Surigao Strait in the Philippines in October 1944 — the last action between battleships in history.) The capsized *Oklahoma* was righted but never repaired. Even the shattered destroyer *Shaw* was sent back into battle. Five ships were completely destroyed by the Japanese attack, and even they yielded parts and materials for re-use in the war. Only the wrecks of the *Arizona* and *Utah* were left in place, as memorials. Even then, the irreparable *Arizona* yielded up two triple gun turrets from her after section for re-use as coastal

(Above) The capsized *Oklahoma* is rolled upright in 1943. (Left) Divers emerge from working inside the shattered *Arizona*. (Right) *Oklahoma* afloat again, with much of her superstructure cut away during salvage. Although she was raised, *Oklahoma* was not repaired — perhaps because there was little need for the old battleship by 1944.

The Investigations: Pointing Fingers and Placing Blame

No military disaster has been as thoroughly investigated as the Pearl Harbor attack; few historical events remain as controversial. The first inquiry was ordered by the President as early as December 18, 1941, and was chaired by US Supreme Court Justice Owen J. Roberts. It finished work on January 23, 1942, gathering 2,173 printed pages of testimony. The Roberts Commission report concluded that Kimmel and Short were guilty of "dereliction of duty," a devastating finding.

Six limited official investigations, including an Army Board and a Navy Court of Inquiry, were conducted in 1944–45, but by far the most thorough inquest was by a Joint Congressional Committee after the war. Regardless of the great victories of the United States and its Allies in 1945, interest in the attack on Pearl Harbor was undiminished when the Committee convened on November 15, with Kentucky Senator Alben W. Barkley in the chair. Hearings ended on May 31, 1946, and the report appeared on July 20 — still the most famous publication on Pearl Harbor, nearly 500 pages long. The Committee gathered 5,560 pages of transcribed testimony in eleven volumes, plus ten volumes of selected exhibits and documentation, plus another nine volumes of extracts from previous inquiries — some 15,000 pages in all.

Public interest was predictably intense at the beginning and the end, and when Kimmel, Short, and a few other key witnesses, such as Stark and Marshall, gave evidence. The Committee stopped short of the Roberts finding of dereliction of duty but identified a series of "errors of judgment" by the two commanders. They neglected warnings from Washington; they did not liaise adequately; they did not maximize reconnaissance; they did not prepare for all possibilities; they did not deploy their forces to repel the attack; and they did not see the significance of information supplied to them. In

(Above) Colonel Rufus C. Bratton, one of the first officers to see intercepts of Japanese messages in 1941, appears as a witness before the Joint Congressional Committee in November 1945.

short, they failed. The War and Navy Departments, but not the State Department, were censured for failing to understand the import of certain items of intelligence and for not forwarding key information to Hawaii.

By giving special attention to the mystery of the "winds code," the Committee unwittingly gave extra ammunition to the "revisionist" industry that was already in full production by the time Congress started work. Just before the attack, the Committee learned, the US Navy deciphered two messages from Tokyo to the Japanese embassy in Washington. These alerted diplomats to a special code of additions to radio weather forecasts that would indicate imminent war with Britain ("west wind, clear"), Russia ("north wind, cloudy") or the United States ("east wind, rain"). Controversy over whether this code was ever used, and then whether it was intercepted by American intelligence, has raged ever since without conclusive proof either way.

So there the matter rests. The "smoking gun" proving that Roosevelt knew in advance, or that Churchill knew but did not tell him, or one, or a combination, of many other conspiracy theories, has still not been found.

In April 1995, Congress sanctioned another inquiry at the request of the Kimmel and Short families. Senator Strom Thurmond, chairman of the Senate Armed Forces Committee, and Representative Floyd Spence, chairman of the House Armed Services Committee, sat for a day and then asked the Department of Defense to conduct a speedy reinvestigation. Undersecretary Edwin Dorn took seven months to reject the request for posthumous restitution of the commanders' rank and reputation. With commendable brevity and clarity, Dorn declared: "As commanders, they were accountable."

artillery. By contrast, every single one of the Japanese warships that took part in the raid was destroyed during the ensuing war. And it started soon. On December 10, the carrier *Enterprise*, on her way back to Pearl Harbor, detected and sank the Japanese submarine *I-70*.

✪

IT TOOK THE UNITED STATES NAVY JUST SIX MONTHS TO TURN THE STRATEGIC TABLES ON the surprise attackers of December 7, 1941. A daring display of initiative began long before the stupendous naval buildup prompted by America's precipitation into World War II gave her an invincible lead. The United States would build a total of 80,000 vessels, from carriers to landing craft, for the Atlantic as well as the Pacific, for her Allies as well as for herself.

Six hours after the attack on Pearl Harbor, Admiral Harold R. Stark, Chief of Naval Operations, issued the order: "Execute unrestricted air and submarine warfare against Japan." These eight words summarize how the Americans won the largest naval campaign ever fought, accompanied as it was by a thrust across the South-West Pacific under General Douglas MacArthur's command.

The new CINCPAC, Admiral Chester W. Nimitz, hoisted his flag on USS *Grayling*, a submarine, there being no battleship available, on December 31. The first US boat, *Gudgeon*, left for Japan's Inland Sea on December 11. On January 27, it became the first American vessel after the US declaration of war to sink an enemy, Japanese submarine *I-173*. The carrier *Yorktown* came via the Panama Canal from the Atlantic to join *Lexington*, *Enterprise* and *Saratoga*.

Filipino and American troops made a heroic and bloody last stand in the Philippines at Bataan and Corregidor before surrendering early in May. This

In what would prove to be an inspired appointment, Admiral Chester W. Nimitz (above) took over the post Kimmel had held, becoming Commander in Chief, Pacific Fleet on December 31, 1941.

concluded the opening stage of the campaign, the phase of apparently unstoppable Japanese conquest. Already at the beginning of February 1942, however, two carriers attacked the Marshall Islands, held by the Japanese. Admiral William F. "Bull" Halsey in *Enterprise* attacked Japanese-occupied Wake Island on February 24, and Marcus Island, 1,000 miles southeast of Tokyo and 2,000 west of Hawaii, on March 4.

On April 18, the new carrier *Hornet*, covered by *Enterprise* in Halsey's just-formed TF-16, launched Lieutenant Colonel James H. Doolittle's sixteen Army B-25 medium bombers to attack Tokyo. Too big to land back on the carrier, the Army planes had to fly on to China afterward. The isolated raid did little damage but caused loss of face in the Japanese high command, which had said it could never happen. The Americans were jubilant at the success of this raid on the Japanese capital.

(Above) B-25 Mitchell bombers under the command of Lieutenant Colonel James Doolittle line the deck of USS *Hornet* before their raid on the Japanese mainland. (Left) Survivors from the *Lexington*, sunk at the battle of the Coral Sea in May 1942. (Right) An American stands guard over Japanese prisoners of war after the Battle of Midway in June 1942. The tide of war had now turned in favor of the United States.

The Doolittle raid — and Japan's previous, multiple success across an 8,000-mile front from Burma in the west to Hawaii in the east — prompted the junta to extend the Empire's perimeter by another complicated naval push southward and westward. The objectives included Port Moresby in New Guinea, Tulagi in the Solomon Islands, Midway, and the US Aleutian Islands off Alaska. The Battle of the Coral Sea northeast of Australia in the first week of May 1942 cost the Americans the *Lexington*, an oiler, and a destroyer, while the *Yorktown* was damaged. The Japanese lost a small carrier and a destroyer, and one fleet carrier was moderately damaged. The Americans' tactical defeat was, however, a strategic one for Japan, which never again made a serious attempt to reinforce New Guinea in strength, or to attack Australia. The southward advance was halted forever, although a long series of bitter battles between large naval and military forces began in the Solomon Islands at the festering outpost of Guadalcanal in August 1942.

The Japanese Navy did occupy Attu and Kiska in the American Aleutians while Admiral Nagumo's four carriers made for Midway, distantly backed by the bulk of the Combined Fleet, led to sea by Yamamoto. A brilliant coup by Pearl Harbor cryptanalyst Commander Joseph J. Rochefort, who finally broke Japanese cipher JN-25, led Admiral Nimitz to risk all by setting a trap for Nagumo in the first week of June 1942. The hastily patched-up *Yorktown* plus *Enterprise* and *Hornet*, with a reinforced Midway acting as an immovable fourth carrier, lay in wait. Halsey was ill; Admiral Raymond Spruance stood in for him. The American carriers, under Rear Admiral Frank Jack Fletcher, sank all four fleet carriers (and one heavy cruiser) — the cutting edge of the Combined Fleet — for the loss of the *Yorktown* and a destroyer.

The Battle of Midway on June 3–7, 1942, was one of the most decisive ever fought. It threw the Japanese onto the defensive just six months after they had decimated the American battlefleet at Pearl Harbor, destroying much of the Japanese Naval Air Force and four out of a total of six fleet carriers. Some of the battles that followed would be larger — but Midway permanently swung the balance of power in the Pacific to the Americans.

PRESIDENT HARRY S. TRUMAN, WHO HAD SUCCEEDED ROOSEVELT ON HIS DEATH IN APRIL 1945, decided to drop the world's first two atomic bombs on Hiroshima and Nagasaki. His motive was to force an early end to the war and save hundreds of thousands of Allied lives that would surely have been lost in an invasion of the Japanese Home Islands. Japan conceded defeat on August 14, 1945.

On September 2, 1945, General Douglas MacArthur, Supreme Commander, Allied Powers, led the surrender ceremony on the broad main deck of USS *Missouri*, the last battleship to be commissioned into the US Navy (June 1944) and the last to fire a shot in anger (in the Gulf War in 1991). Now the great ship, last of the dreadnoughts, is a floating museum, proudly standing guard on Battleship Row over the grave of USS *Arizona* — the two warships symbolizing the beginning, and the end, of an epic conflict.

Japan Surrenders

On August 14, 1945, shortly after the bombing of Hiroshima and Nagasaki, Japan indicated to the Allies that it had had enough. On September 2, 1945, the formal surrender ceremony took place in Tokyo Bay aboard the American battleship *Missouri*, surrounded by a vast allied armada. (Top) The representatives of the Japanese government are received aboard. (Above) General Douglas MacArthur signs the surrender documents. Behind him stand General Wainwright, American commander in the Philippines, and General Percival, who commanded the British forces in Malaya. The long chain of events set in play by the attack on Pearl Harbor nearly four years before was finally over.

"Remember Pearl Harbor"

As Admiral Yamamoto had feared, the attack on Pearl Harbor awakened the sleeping giant, America. And the manner of the attack — which Americans regarded as a treacherous, underhanded assault — aroused the country's patriotism to unimagined heights. The phrase "Remember Pearl Harbor" immediately became a rallying cry, as young men flocked to enlist and those who stayed behind bought war bonds and volunteered in various ways to help the war effort. So deeply did the phrase become embedded in the American psyche that it spawned an avalanche of Pearl Harbor memorabilia. The words "Remember Pearl Harbor" soon decorated items ranging from greeting cards and license plates to comic books, jewelry, postage stamps — and even underwear. One fetching pair of bloomers exhorted the lucky viewer: "Don't Get Caught With Your Pants Down. Remember Pearl Harbor." Today, sixty years after the "day of infamy," Pearl Harbor collectibles are more popular than ever.

LET'S GO AMERICANS

REMEMBER PEARL HARBOR

REMEMBER PEARL HARBOR

DONALD M. BARRY

A REPUBLIC PIC...

REMEMBER PEARL HARBOR

WORDS BY DON REID
MUSIC BY DON REID and SAMMY KAYE

REPUBLIC MUSIC CORPORATION

Lest We Forget
That Historical Fateful Day
December 7, 1941
Remember Pearl Harbor

"So the Way
of Our Life
Shall Continue"

LIBERTY UNDER GOD

REMEMBER PEARL HARBOR

I BOUGHT MY PEARL HARBOR DAY BOND

REMEMBER PEARL HARBOR
KEEP 'EM FLYING

(Opposite) This imposing poster uses the image of the burning *Arizona* to dramatic effect. When it came to "Remembering Pearl Harbor," there were many ways to do it. One could opt for a simple felt pennant (top) or a brooch in the shape of a plane (top right). The entertainment industry quickly jumped on the Pearl Harbor bandwagon with a quickie movie (poster, center left) and a hit song (center, middle). While many mementos were straightforward and simple, like these patriotic buttons and fringed pillow cover (bottom left), others invoked religious iconography (center, right) or wartime jingoism (right) to make their point.

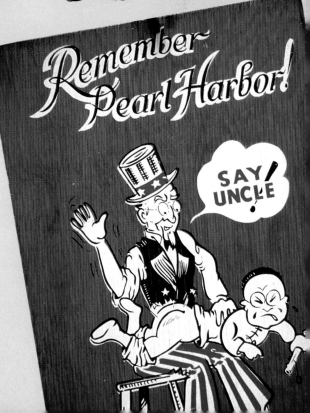

Remember Pearl Harbor!

SAY UNCLE!

(Left) It climaxed with the raid on Pearl Harbor, but director Fred Zinnemann's *From Here to Eternity* was really a story of prewar military life — with Oscar-winning performances by Deborah Kerr, Donna Reed, Montgomery Clift, Burt Lancaster, and Frank Sinatra. (Above left) *I Bombed Pearl Harbor* was a new generation's introduction to the story of the attack. (Above right and below) The graphic battle scenes in *Tora! Tora! Tora!* lasted nearly as long as the original attack.

Hollywood's Pearl Harbor

The wreckage was still smoldering when the first film crews arrived at Pearl Harbor. Members of Hollywood director John Ford's naval film unit — recruited by Ford before the United States even entered the war — showed up a week after the attack. The resulting short, *December 7*, won an Academy Award for best documentary in 1943. But people didn't know that the successful film was a scaled-down version of a far grander work.

That film starred Walter Huston as Uncle Sam and Harry Davenport as Mr. C (for Conscience), and included the documentary footage from Pearl Harbor as well as scenes shot in Arlington Cemetery — with a voice-over featuring the war dead in conversation (sailor killed at Pearl Harbor to cynical shade of Great War doughboy: "I'm putting my bets on the Roosevelts, the Churchills, the Stalins, and the Chiang Kai-Sheks.") Ford's original movie pointed fingers and assigned blame for the debacle. Not surprisingly, it was shelved. Only one print exists in the National Archives.

Perhaps because of the sheer scale of the attack, most filmmakers treated Pearl Harbor obliquely. Howard Hawks' great *Air Force* (1943), starring John Garfield, focused on a B-17 crew flying into Oahu that morning, but moved on from the islands quickly. *From Here to Eternity*, which won eight Academy Awards in 1953, touched on the battle but was mostly a depiction of life before the attack.

In the post-war period, the first real attempt to tell the complete story was, oddly, Japanese. *I Bombed Pearl Harbor* (1961) dealt with the attack as well as the fate of the Japanese carriers at Midway. Dubbed into English, it introduced the baby-boomer generation to the story.

The year 1970 saw the release of *Tora! Tora! Tora!*, an American-Japanese co-production that told the story from both sides. Exhaustingly accurate, with an attack sequence nearly as long as the original battle, *Tora! Tora! Tora!* was a success in Japan but a box office failure in North America. At a then-exorbitant $25 million, wags noted that it cost Hollywood more to film the attack than it had for Japan to carry it out.

In the run-up to the sixtieth anniversary of Pearl Harbor, Hollywood again focused its lens on December 7, 1941. Released for Memorial Day weekend 2001, director Jerry Bruckheimer's *Pearl Harbor* features the most spectacular cinematic version of the battle ever.

(Left) Director John Ford won a 1943 Academy Award for his Pearl Harbor short, *December 7*. (Above) One of the most spectacular films of its day, director Richard Fleischer's 1970 epic, *Tora! Tora! Tora!*, told both sides of the Pearl Harbor story. In these scenes from the film, the Japanese hit Wheeler Field (top) and an American battleship suffers a direct hit (middle and bottom).

The Legacy

"We have awakened a sleeping giant and instilled in him a terrible resolve."

— Admiral Isoroku Yamamoto

(Previous page) The USS *Arizona* Memorial today. (Above) A National Park Service ranger raises a flag over the Memorial. (Below) Although most of *Arizona* is submerged, the barbette that once held the battleship's number two turret remains above water. (Opposite) Today, sixty years after the *Arizona* sank, oil continues to seep from deep inside the battleship.

T HE PEARL HARBOR ATTACK WAS CON- ceived by Admiral Yamamoto, planned by the Imperial Japanese Navy, and executed with panache and dedication by the airmen of Admiral Nagumo's Mobile Force. It was all the more likely to succeed given the US administration's determination, in Secretary Stimson's words, that "if hostilities cannot be avoided, the United States desires that Japan commit the first overt act." Yet it was a strategic failure for Japan. While it knocked out the US battlefleet, it missed the aircraft carriers that were the foundation of America's ultimate victory. And it failed to destroy Oahu as the US Navy's main base in the Pacific, from where it dominates that ocean to this day. Genda and Fuchida were among those Japanese who saw these shortcomings at the time and pressed for a second strike. Nagumo's decision not to do so may have been Japan's biggest strategic mistake of the war.

The marching song "Remember Pearl Harbor" by Don Reid and Sammy Kaye swept across the country within weeks of the raid. Though the tune is now forgotten, the events of December 7, 1941, have not been. The attack remains America's most devastating single lost battle by far. But it was — remains — more than that. America was changed in those two brief hours. Division gave way to unity, isolationism to engagement. Today's military, economic, and cultural superpower was born in that raid. When reflecting on the legacy of Pearl Harbor — the old photos, the accounts of courage, perhaps some commemorative medal or poster — it should not be forgotten that the modern United States, indeed, the modern world, is also part of the legacy of Pearl Harbor. It is a catastrophe well remembered.

THE FINAL TOLL

In the first hours of America's Pacific War, the nation suffered one of its worst wartime losses: 2,390 men, women, and children were killed in the attack. These pages list persons, military and civilian, who died as a result of the attack or were killed later that day in the performance of their duties. The listing of servicemen is by branch of service and duty station. The list of civilians is by location. Sailors and marines killed on board the USS *Arizona* are identified beginning on page 167. Medal of Honor recipients are listed on page 171. The list of Japanese personnel killed in the attack appears on page 171.

Civilian
✪

Ewa

Yaeko Lillian Oda, 6

Francisco Tacderan, 34

Honolulu

John Kalauwae Adams, 18	Joseph Kanehoa Adams, 50
Nancy Masako Arakaki, 8	Patrick Kahamokupuni Chong, 30
Matilda Kaliko Faufata, 12	Emma Gonsalves, 34
Ai Harada, 54	Kisa Hatate, 41
Fred Masayoshi Higa, 21	Jackie Yoneto Hirasaki, 8
Jitsuo Hirasaki, 48	Robert Yoshito Hirasaki, 3
Shirley Kinue Hirasaki, 2	Paul S. Inamine, 19
Robert Seiko Izumi, 25	David Kahookele, 23
Edward Koichi Kondo, 19	Peter Souza Lopes, 33
George Jay Manganelli, 14	Joseph McCabe, Sr., 43
Masayoshi Nagamine, 27	Frank Ohashi, 29
Hayako Ohta, 19	Janet Yumiko Ohta, 3 months
Kiyoko Ohta, 21	Barbara June Ornellas, 8
Gertrude Ornellas, 16	James Takao Takefuji, aka Koba, 20
Yoshio Tokusato, 19	Hisao Uyeno, 20
Alice White, 42	Eunice Wilson, 7 months

John Rodgers Airport

Robert H. Tyce, 38

Kaneohe Naval Air Station

Kamiko Kookano, 35

Isaac William Lee, 21

Pearl City

Rowena Kamohaulani Foster, 3

Wahiawa

Chip Soon Kim, 66

Richard Masaru Soma, 22

Waipahu

Tomoso Kimura, 19

Honolulu Fire Department
✪

Hickam Field

John Carriera, 51

Thomas Samuel Macy, 59

Harry Tuck Lee Pang, 30

Federal Government Employees
✪

Hickam Field

August Akina, 37

Philip Ward Eldred, 36
Virgil P. Rahel

Pearl Harbor

Tai Chung Loo, 19

Red Hill

Daniel LaVerne, 25

United States Army
✪

Camp Malakole

F BATTERY 251ST COAST ARTILLERY (AA)
These soldiers were shot down by Japanese planes over John Rodgers Airport while taking flying lessons.

Henry C. Blackwell, Sgt

Clyde C. Brown, Cpl

Warren D. Rasmussen, Sgt

Fort Barrette

C BATTERY 15TH COAST ARTILLERY
Joseph A. Medlen, Spl

Fort Kamehameha

C BATTERY 41ST COAST ARTILLERY
Claude L. Bryant, Cpt   Eugene B. Bubb, Pvt
Oreste DaTorre, PFC   Donat G. Duquette, Jr., Pvt

C BATTERY 55TH COAST ARTILLERY
Edward F. Sullivan, Pvt

Fort Shafter

E BATTERY 64TH COAST ARTILLERY (AA)
Arthur A. Favreau, PFC

Fort Weaver

97TH COAST ARTILLERY (AA)
William G. Sylvester, 1st Lt
Killed in a car while driving through Hickam Field

Schofield Barracks

L COMPANY 21ST INFANTRY
Paul J. Fadon, Sgt
Killed in a truck accident 10 miles north of Schofield Barracks

HQ BTY 63RD FIELD ARTILLERY
Theodore J. Lewis, Cpt

89TH FIELD ARTILLERY
Walter R. French, Pvt

A BATTERY 98TH FIELD ARTILLERY
Conrad Kujawa, PFC
Killed in an accidental electrocution

D COMPANY 298TH INFANTRY
Torao Migita, Pvt
Killed in downtown Honolulu by "friendly fire"

USS Arizona Memorial

Source: Official website of the National Parks Service / Arizona memorial (Pearl Harbor casualties)

United States Army Air Force

✪

Bellows Field

44TH PURSUIT SQUADRON
Hans C. Christiansen, 2d Lt   George A. Whiteman, 2d Lt

Hickam Field

4TH RECONNAISSANCE SQUADRON
Lawrence R. Carlson, Pvt   Donald F. Meahger, Cpl
Louis Schleifer, PFC

HQ SQD 5TH BOMBARDMENT GROUP
George P. Bolan, SSgt   Richard A. Dickerson, Cpl
Alfred Hays, Pvt   Richard E. Livingston, Pvt
George M. Martin, Jr., Sgt

7TH AIRCRAFT SQUADRON (WEATHER)
Harold W. Borgelt, Cpl   Daniel A. Dyer, Jr., TSgt
Sherman Levine, PFC   James M. Topalian, Cpl

HQ SQD 11TH BOMBARDMENT GROUP
Robert L. Avery, Cpl   Robert S. Brown, Pvt
Edward J. Cashman, TSgt   Donal V. Chapman, PFC
Monroe M. Clark, SSgt   Robert H. Gooding, Pvt
James A. Horner, PFC   George F. Howard, PFC
Lawrence P. Lyons, Jr., Pvt   Wallae R. Martin, 1st Sgt
William W. Merithew, PFC   George A. Moran, Pvt
Herman C. Reuss, TSgt   Robert M. Richey, 1st Lt
Harry E. Smith, Pvt   Edward F. Vernick, PFC
Marion H. Zaczkiewicz, PFC

HQ SQD 17TH AIR BASE GROUP
Jerry M. Angelich, Pvt   Malcolm J. Brummwell, 1st Lt
Jack A. Downs, Pvt   Paul R. Eichelberger, Pvt
Arnold E. Field, Pvt   Joseph Jedrysik, Pvt
Andrew J. Kinder, Pvt   Herbert E. McLaughlin, Pvt
Emmett E. Morris, Cpl   Joseph F. Nelles, PFC
Willard C. Orr, PFC   Halvor E. Rogness, Pvt
Leo H. Surrells, Pvt

18TH AIR BASE SQUADRON
Joseph Bush, Pvt   John H. Couhig, Pvt
Harold C. Elyard, SSgt   Willard E. Fairchild, Pvt
Paul V. Fellman, SSgt   Homer E. Ferris, TSgt
Stuart H. Fiander, Pvt   James J. Gleason, PFC
Otto C. Klein, Pvt   Harry W. Lord, Jr., Pvt
Joseph Malatak, Pvt   Russell M. Penny, Pvt
Allen G. Rae, Pvt   George J. Smith, PFC
Elmer W. South, Pvt   Hermann K. Tibbets, Jr., Pvt
George W. Tuckerman, Pvt   Martin Vanderelli, Pvt
Walter H. Wardigo, Pvt   Lawton J. Woodworth, Pvt
Thomas M. Wright, Pvt   Virgil J. Young, Pvt

HQ SQD 18TH BOMBARDMENT WING
Garland C. Anderson, Pvt   Manfred C. Anderson, Pvt
Gordon R. Bennett, Jr., Pvt   Frank G. Boswell, Pvt
Frank B. Cooper, Pvt   John E. Cruthirds, PFC
Robert C. Duff, Jr., Pvt   Lyle O. Edwards, Pvt
Russell E. Gallagher, Pvt   James E. Gossard, Jr., PFC
Johon S. Greene, 1st Lt   Earl A. Hood, Pvt
Theodore K. Joyner, Pvt   Edmund B. Lepper, Sgt
Durward A. Meadows, PFC   LaVerne J. Needham, Cpl
Paul L. Staton, Pvt   Anderson G. Tennison, PFC

19TH TRANSPORT SQUADRON
William T. Anderson, Cpl   William T. Blakley, Pvt

Hickam Field Memorial

Russell C. Defenbaugh, Pvt   Joseph H. Guttmann, Pvt
John J. Horan, Pvt   Carl A. Johnson, Pvt
Olaf A. Johnson, PFC   Doyle Kimmey, SSgt
James I. Lewis, PFC   William E. McAbee, PFC
Stanley A. McLeod, Sgt   Walter D. Zuckoff, Pvt

22ND MATERIEL SQUADRON
Arthur F. Boyle, Pvt   Billy O. Brandt, SSgt
Rennie V. Brower, Jr., Pvt   William J. Brownlee, Pvt
Brooks J. Brubaker, Pvt   Weldon C. Burlison, Pvt
Leroy R. Church, Pvt   Jack H. Feldman, Pvt
Leo E. A. Gagne, Pvt   Allen E. W. Goudy, Pvt
William E. Hasenfuss, Jr.,PFC   James R. Johnson, Pvt
Robert H. Johnson, Pvt   Marion E. King, Jr., Pvt
Roderick O. Klubertanz, Pvt   John H. Mann, SSgt
James J. McClintock, PFC   Horace A. Messam, PFC
Victor L. Meyers, Pvt   Edwin N. Mitchell, Cpl
Thomas F. Philipsky, PFC   William F. Shields, Pvt
Ralph S. Smith, PFC   John B. Sparks, PFC
Merton I. Staples, Pvt   Jerome J. Szematowicz, PFC
William F. Timmerman, Pvt   Ernest M. Walker, Jr., Pvt

23RD BOMBARDMENT SQUADRON
Lee I. Clendenning, PFC   Richard L. Coster, Pvt
Byron G. Elliott, Pvt   William Hislop, PFC
Howard N. Lusk, Pvt   Lionel J. Moorhead, PFC

23RD MATERIEL SQUADRON
Francis E. Campiglia, Pvt   Herbert B. Martin, 1Sgt
Joseph G. Moser, Pvt   Frank St. E. Posey, TSgt
Raymond E. Powell, TSgt   William T. Rhodes, PFC
Maurice J. St. Germain, Pvt   James E. Strickland, Jr., Pvt
Joseph S. Zappala, Pvt   Walter J. Zuschlag, SSgt

26TH BOMBARDMENT SQUADRON
Felix Bonnie, SSgt   Clarence A. Conant, Pvt
Frank J. DePolis, SSgt   Patrick I. Finney, Cpl
Elwood R. Gummerson, SSgt   Vincent J. Kechner, Pvt
Robert H. Markley, 2d Lt   Jay E. Pietzsch, 2d Lt
Antonio S. Tafoya, Cpl   Robert H. Westbrook, Jr., Pvt

31ST BOMBARDMENT SQUADRON
Jack W. Fox, PFC   Frank J. Lango, Pvt
William M. Northway, Pvt   Felix S. Wegrzyn, Pvt

38TH RECONNAISSANCE SQUADRON
William R. Schick, 1st Lt

42ND BOMBARDMENT SQUADRON
Leland V. Beasley, Pvt   William Coyne, Jr., PFC
Eugene B. Denson, PFC   Robert R. Garrett, Cpl
Charles I. Hrusecky, Pvt   Joseph N. Jencuis, Pvt
Robert R. Kelley, PFC   Hal H. Perry, Jr., Pvt
Carey K. Stockwell, Pvt

50TH RECONNAISSANCE SQUADRON
Ralph Alois, SSgt   Louis H. Dasenbrock, Pvt
John T. Haughey, Pvt   Clarence E. Hoyt, PFC
Henry J. Humphrey, SSgt   Lester H. Libolt, Cpl
Harell K. Mattox, PFC   William H. Offutt, Cpl

72ND BOMBARDMENT SQUADRON
Edward R. Hughes, Pvt   John J. Kohl, PFC
George Price, Pvt

1ST PHOTO GROUP, ATTACHED TO FERRY COMMAND
These airmen, originally attached to the 44th Bomb Group, arrived in Hawaii two days prior to the attack to outfit their plane for a secret photo mission. They were killed on the ground and their B-24 was destroyed near Hangar 15.
Louis G. Moslener, Jr., 2d Lt   Daniel J. Powloski, Pvt

Wheeler Field

46TH PURSUIT SQUADRON
Donald D. Plant, Pvt   Gordon H. Sterling, Jr., 2d Lt

47TH PURSUIT SQUADRON
John I. Dains, 2d Lt
Shot down by "friendly fire"

72ND PURSUIT SQUADRON
Edward J. Burns, 1st Sgt   Malachy J. Cashen, Cpl
Dean W. Cebert, Pvt   William C. Creech, PFC
James Everett, SSgt   Paul B. Free, SSgt
Joseph E. Good, SSgt   James E. Guthrie, SSgt
Robert L. Hull, Pvt   George G. Leslie, Pvt
John A. Price, SSgt

73RD PURSUIT SQUADRON
James M. Barksdale, SSgt

78TH PURSUIT SQUADRON
Vincent M. Horan, Cpl   Morris E. Stacey, Sgt

United States Marine Corps

✪

USS California *BB-44, Battleship*

John A. Blount, Jr., PFC   Roy E. Lee, Jr., Pvt
Shelby C. Shook, Pvt   Earl D. Wallen, PFC

USS Helena *CL-50, Light Cruiser*

George E. Johnson, PFC

USS Nevada *BB-36, Battleship*

Thomas A. Britton, Cpl   Francis C. Heath, PFC
Orveil V. King, Jr., PFC   Jack L. Lunsford, PFC
Edward F. Morrissey, PFC   Keith V. Smith, Pvt
Richard I. Trujillo, PFC

USS Oklahoma BB-37, Battleship

Marley R. Arthurholtz, PFC	Waldean Black, Pvt
Walter L. Collier, PFC	Alva J. Cremean, PFC
Elmer E. Drefahl, Cpl	Harry H. Gaver, Jr., 2d Lt
Ted Hall, Pvt	Otis W. Henry, Pvt
Robert K. Holmes, PFC	Vernon P. Keaton, Pvt
John F. Middleswart, PFC	Robert H. Peak, Pvt
Raymond Pennington, Pvt	Charles R. Taylor, PFC

USS Pennsylvania BB-38, Battleship

Thomas N. Barron, Cpl	Morris E. Nations, Cpl
Floyd D. Stewart, PFC	Patrick P. Tobin, PFC
Jesse C. Vincent, Jr., Cpl	George H. Wade, Jr., PFC

Ewa Marine Corps Air Station

MARINE AIRCRAFT GROUP 21 HEADQUARTERS AND SERVICE SQUADRON 21
William E. Lutschan, Jr., Sgt

SCOUTING-BOMBING SQUADRON 231
William G. Turner, Pvt

SCOUTING-BOMBING SQUADRON 232
Edward S. Lawrence, PFC

UTILITY SQUADRON 252
Carlo A. Micheletto, Sgt

United States Navy
✪

USS California BB-44, Battleship

Howard L. Adkins, F1c	Moses A. Allen, MAtt1c
Thomas B. Allen, GM2c	Wilbur H. Bailey, Sea1c
Glen Baker, Sea2c	James W. Ball, F2c
Harold W. Bandemer, Sea1c	Michael L. Bazetti, Sea1c
Albert Q. Beal, RM2c	Thomas S. Beckwith, SF3c
Henry W. Blankenship, PhM1c	Edward D. Bowden, F2c
Robert K. Bowers, Ens (VO-2)	Robert L. Brewer, Sea1c
Samuel J. Bush, MAtt1c	James W. Butler, F2c
Elmer L. Carpenter, BM1c	Cullen B. Clark, F1c
Francis E. Cole, Msmth2c	Kenneth J. Cooper, FC3c
Herbert S. Curtis, Jr., Sea2c	Lloyd H. Cutrer, Sea2c
Edward H. Davis, SK1c	John W. Deetz, GM3c
Marshall L. Dompier, SK2c	Norman W. Douglas, Sea1c
Guy Dugger, F1c	Billie J. Dukes, Sea1c
Thomas R. Durning, Jr., Sea2c	Robert W. Ernest, Sea2c
Alfred J. Farley, Sea2c	Marvin L. Ferguson, Jr., AS
Stanley C. Galaszewski, Sea2c	Robert S. Garcia, SK3c
Thomas J. Gary, Sea2c	George H. Gilbert, Ens
Tom Gilbert, Sea1c	Helmer A. Hanson, Sea2c
Gilbert A. Henderson, MAtt2c	John A. Hildebrand, Jr., F1c
Merle C. J. Hillman, PhM2c	Paul E. Holley, Sea1c
Richard F. Jacobs, SF3c	Ira W. Jeffrey, Ens
Melvin G. Johnson, RM3c	Ernest Jones, MAtt3c
Herbert C. Jones, Ens	Harry Kaufman, BM1c
Arlie G. Keener, SK3c	Harry W. Kramer, F1c
John T. Lancaster, PhM3c	Donald C. V. Larsen, RM3c
John E. Lewis, SK1c	James E. London, SK1c
Howard E. Manges, FC3c	John W. Martin, F3c
George V. McGraw, F1c	Clyde C. McMeans, Sea1c
Aaron L. McMurtrey, Sea1c	James W. Milner, F1c
James D. Minter, Sea2c	Bernard J. Mirello, Sea1c
William A. Montgomery, GM3c	Marlyn W. Nelson, F2c
Wayne E. Newton, Sea1c	June W. Parker, QM3c
Kenneth M. Payne, Sea1c	George E. Pendarvis, F3c

Lewis W. Pitts, Jr., Sea2c	Alexsander J. Przybysz, Prtr2c
Roy A. Pullen, Sea2c	Edward S. Racisz, Sea1c
Thomas J. Reeves, CRM (PA)	Joseph L. Richey, Ens (VO-2)
Edwin H. Ripley, Sea2c	Earl R. Roberts, Sea1c
Alfred A. Rosenthal, RM3c	Joe B. Ross, RM2c
Frank W. Royse, RM3c	Morris F. Saffell, F1c
Robert R. Scott, MM1c	Erwin L. Searle, GM3c
Russell K. Shelly, Jr., Mus2c	Frank L. Simmons, MAtt2c
Tceollyar Simmons, Sea2c	Lloyd G. Smith, Sea2c
Gordon W. Stafford, Sea2c	Leo Stapler, MAtt1c
Charles E. Sweany, EM1c	Edward F. Szurgot, SK3c
Frank P. Treanor, RM3c	Pete Turk, Sea2c
George V. Ulrich, F1c	George E. Vining, MAtt2c
David Walker, MAtt3c	Milton S. Wilson, F3c
Steven J. Wodarski, Sea1c	John C. Wydila, SF3c

USS Chew DD-106, Destroyer

Mathew J. Agola, Sea2	Clarence A. Wise, F3c
Killed on the Pennsylvania	

USS Curtiss AV-4, Seaplane Tender

Joseph I. Caro, F1c	Lee H. Duke, Sea2c
Clifton E. Edmonds, Sea1c	John W. Frazier, Cox
Nickolas S. Ganas, Sea2c	George H. Guy, Sea2c
Kenneth J. Hartley, F1c	Edward S. Haven, Jr., Sea1c
Anthony Hawkins, Jr., MAtt2c	Thomas Hembree, AS
Andrew King, AS	Robert S. Lowe, Sea2c
James E. Massey, AS	Maurice Mastrototaro, Sea1c
Jesse K. Milbourne, AS	Dean B. Orwick, RM2c
William J. Powell, MAtt2c	Wilson A. Rice, Sea1c
Howard A. Rosenau, Sea2c	Benjamin Schlect, RM2c
Joseph Sperling, SF1c	

USS Dobbin AD-3, Destroyer Tender

J. W. Baker, TM3c	Howard F. Carter, Cox
Roy A. Gross, F1c	Andrew M. Marze, GM1c
	Killed on the Pennsylvania

USS Downes DD-375, Destroyer

James E. Bailey, RM3c	Benjamin L. Brown, Sea2c
Marvin J. Clapp, SC3c	Thomas W. Collins, F3c
Edward C. Daly, Cox	Albert J. Hitrik, F2c
George E. Jones, Rm3c	John A. Marshall, WT2c
Nolan E. Pummill, MM2c	William H. Silva, Sea2c
Perry W. Strickland, Sea1c	James Vinson, F3c

USS Enterprise CV-6, Aircraft Carrier

At the time of the attack, the Enterprise *was at sea, about 200 miles due west of Oahu.*

SCOUTING SQUADRON SIX
These aviators arrived over Oahu during the attack and were shot down by the Japanese.

Mitchell Cohn, RM3c	Fred J. Ducolon, Cox
Manuel Gonzalez, Ens	Leonard J. Kozelek, RM3c
William C. Miller, Rm1c	Signey Pierce, Rm3c
John H. L. Vogt, Jr., Ens	Walter M. Willis, Ens

FIGHTING SQUADRON SIX
These aviators were shot down by "friendly fire" in an attempt to make a night landing at Ford Island NAS.

Eric Allen, Jr., Lt. (jg)	Frederick F. Hebel, Lt. (jg)
Herbert H. Menges, Ens	

USS Helena CL-50, Light Cruiser

Salvatore J. Albanese, F2c	Thomas E. Aldridge, Sea2c

Robert A. Arnesen, F1c	Loren L. Beardsley, EM3c
Regis J. Bodecker, Y1c	William J. Carter, Sea2c
Luther E. Cisco, Sea2c	Allen A. Davis, F3c
Ernest B. Dickens, F2c	Richard H. Dobbins, EM2c
Robert N. Edling, RM3c	Leland E. Erbes, F2c
Robert J. Flannery, FC3c	Eugene D. Fuzi, FC3c
Arthur J. Gardner, WT2c	Robert D. Greenwald, Sea1c
Arvel C. Hines, Sea2c	Donald W. Johnson, Sea2c
Ernest G. Kuzee, Sea1c	Carl R. Love, Sea2c
Marvin W. Mayo, FC2c	Orville R. Minix, Sea1c
Edo Morincelli, MM2c	Hugh K. Naff, Sea2c
John C. Pensyl, GM2c	Joe O. Powers, SK3c
Ralph W. Thompson, F3c	Edward B. Uhlig, Sea2c
John J. Urban, MM2c	Benjamin F. Vassar, Sea2c
Hoge C. Venable, Jr., SK2c	Oswald C. Wohl, Sea2c
Michael C. Yugovich, EM2c	

USS Maryland BB-46, Battleship

Claire R. Brier, MM2c	Howard D. Crow, Ens
James B. Ginn, Lt.(jg)(VO-4)	Warren H. McCutcheon, Sea2c
Killed in an air crash 10 miles west of Barbers Pt.	

USS Nevada BB-36, Battleship

Arnold L. Anderson, Sea1c	Zoilo Aquino, MAtt1c
James R. Bingham, Sea2c	Herman Bledsoe, MAtt2c
Lyle L. Briggs, EM2c	Harold J. Christopher, Ens
Joseph W. Cook, GM3c	Leon J. Corbin, GM1c
Leo P. Cotner, Sea2c	Frederick C. Davis, Ens (VO-1)
Lonnie W. Dukes, Sea1c	Edward W. Echols, Cox
Harry L. Edwards, Sea1c	George L. Faddis, GM3c
Kay I. Fugate, Sea1c	Samuel M. Gantner, BM2c
Thomas R. Giles, EM3c	Herman A. Goetsch, Sea1c
Arthur K. Gullachson, Sea2c	Johnnie W. Hallmark, Sea1c
Charles W. Harker, FC3c	Gerald L. Heim, Sea2c
Edwin J. Hill, Chf Bosn	Edgar E. Hubner, Sea1c
Robert C. Irish, Sea2c	Flavous B. M. Johnson, GM3c
Kenneth T. Lamons, BM2c	Wilbur T. Lipe, Sea2c
John K. Luntta, Sea1c	Andres F. Mafnas, MAtt1c
Dale L. Martin, SC1c	Frazier Mayfield, MAtt1c
Lester F. McGhee, Sea1c	Edward L. McGuckin, Sea1c
William F. Neuendorf, Jr., Sea1c	Alwyn B. Norvelle, CSK (AA)
Elmer M. Patterson, OC2c	Eugene E. Peck, Sea2c
Mark C. Robison, MAtt1c	Emil O. Ronning, Cox
Harvey G. Rushford, Sea2c	Herbert C. Schwarting, Sea1c
Donald R. Shaum, Sea1c	Adolfo Solar, BM1c
Herman A. Spear, Sea1c	Delbert J. Spencer, Sea1c
George J. Stembrosky, Sea1c	Charles E. Strickland, Sea1c
Lee V. Thunhorst, Sea2c	Ivan I. Walton, Cox

USS Oklahoma BB-37, Battleship

Marvin B. Adkins, GM3c	Willard H. Aldridge, Sea1c
Hugh R. Alexander, Lt. Comdr	Stanley W. Allen, Ens (VO-1)
Hal J. Allison, F2c	Leon Arickx, Sea1c
Kenneth B. Armstrong, Mldr1c	Daryle E. Artley, QM2c
John C. Auld, Sea2c	John A. Austin, Chf Carp
Walter H. Backman, RM2c	Gerald J. Bailey, Sea1c
Robert E. Bailey, SF3c	Wilbur F. Ballance, Sea1c
Layton T. Banks, Cox	Leroy K. Barber, F1c
Malcolm J. Barber, F1c	Randolph H. Barber, F2c
Cecil E. Barncord, EM3c	Wilber C. Barrett, Sea2c
Harold E. Bates, F1c	Ralph C. Battles, F2c
Earl P. Baum, Sea1c	Howard W. Bean, RM3c
Walter S. Belt, Jr., F1c	Robert J. Bennett, F3c
Harding C. Blackburn, Y3c	William E. Blanchard, Bmkr1c
Clarence A. Blaylock, F3c	Leo Blitz, MM2c
Rudolph Blitz, F1c	John G. Bock Jr., Sea2c
Paul L. Boemer, Cox	James B. Booe, Cbmster

James B. Boring, F2c
Lawrence A. Boxrucker, F2c
Carl M. Bradley, F2c
Jack A. Breedlove, FC3c
William Brooks, Sea1c
William G. Bruesewitz, Sea1c
Earl G. Burch, Bkr3c
Millard Burk, Jr., Sea1c
Archie Callahan, Jr., MAtt2c
William V. Campbell, Sea2c
Harold F. Carney, MM1c
Edward E. Casinger, F2c
Carles R. Casto, F1c
James T. Chesire, CPhM(PA)
David Clark, Jr., Sea2c
Hubert P. Clement, FC1c
George A. Coke, Sea1c
John G. Connolly, Chf Pay Clk

Ralph M. Boudreaux, MAtt1c
Raymond D. Boynton, Sea2c
Orix V. Brandt, Sea1c
Randall W. Brewer, MAtt1c
Wesley J. Brown, F1c
James R. Buchanan, MM2c
Oliver K. Burger, WT1c
Rodger C. Butts, SC1c
Raymond R. Camery, F1c
Murry R. Cargile, Sea1c
Joseph W. Carroll, F2c
Biacio Casola, Sea1c
Richard E. Casto, F2c
Patrick L. Chess, SF3c
Gerald L. Clayton, SK2c
Floyd F. Clifford, Sea2c
James E. Collins, Sea1c
Keefe R. Connolly, HA1c

Benjamin E. Gilliard, MAtt1c
Daryl H. Goggin, Mach
Charles C. Gomez, Jr., Sea2c
Clifford G. Goodwin, Sea1c
Duff Gordon, CMsmth
Wesley E. Graham, Sea1c
Thomas E. Griffith, RM3c
Vernon N. Grow, Sea2c
William I. Gurganus, CEM (AA)
Hubert P. Hall, Sea2c
Harold W. Ham, MM2c
Eugene P. Hann, GM3c
George Hanson, MM1c
Charles H. Harris, EM3c
Louis E. Harris, Jr., Mus2c
Harold L. Head, Sea2c
William F. Hellstern, GM2c
Jimmie L. Henrichsen, Sea2c

Arthur Glenn, MM1c
Jack R. Goldwater, RM3c
George M. Gooch, EM3c
Robert Goodwin, SC3c
Claude O. Gowey, F1c
Arthur M. Grand Pre, F1c
Edgar D. Gross, WT2c
Daniel L. Guisinger, Jr., Sea1c
William F. Gusie, FC3c
Robert E. Halterman, Sea1c
Dale R. Hamlin, GM3c
Francis L. Hannon, SF3c
Robert J. Harr, F1c
Daniel F. Harris, CFC (PA)
Albert E. Hayden, CEM (PA)
Robert W. Headington, Sea1c
Floyd D. Helton, Sea2c
William E. Henson, Jr., Sea2c

Gerald G. Lehman, F3c
Lionel W. Lescault, Bgmstr2c
John H. Lindsley, F3c
Clarence M. Lockwood, WT2c
Vernon T. Luke, MM1c
Howard S. Magers, Sea2c
Algeo V. Malfante, SF2c
Henri C. Mason, Mus1c
Edwin B. McCabe WT1c
James O. McDonald, F1c
Hale McKissack, Sea1c
Earl R. Melton, MM1c
Archie T. Miles, MM2c
Charles A. Montgomery, RM3c
Ray H. Myers, Sea2c
Elmer D. Nail, F1c
Don O. Neher, EM3c
Sam D. Nevill, Y3c
Carl Nichols, Sea2c
Frank E. Nicoles, F1c
Laverne A. Nigg, Sea2c
Charles E. Nix, SM3c
Charles R. Ogle, F1c
Jarvis G. Outland, F1c
Alphard S. Owsley, EM3c
James Palides, Jr., Mus2c
Wilferd D. Palmer, Sea2c
Isaac Parker, MAtt3c
Walter R. Pentico, Sea2c
Charles F. Perdue, SF1c
Milo E. Phillips, WT1c
Gerald H. Pirtle, F1c
Herbert J. Poindexter, Jr., Sea1c
Robert L. Pribble, FC3c
Lewis B. Pride, Jr., Ens
Paul S. Raimond, Sea1c
Dan E. Reagan, F1c
Irvin F. Rice, RM3c
Clyde Ridenour, Jr., RM3c
Russell C. Roach, Sea1c
Harold W. Roesch, Sea1c
Joseph C. Rouse, Sea1c
Edmund T. Ryan, Y3c
Kenneth H. Sampson, Sea1c
Charles L. Saunders, Sea2c
John E. Savidge, Sea1c
Walter F. Schleiter, F1c
Aloysius H. Schmitt, Lt.(ChC)
John H. Schoonover, PhM1c
Chester E. Seaton, F1c
William L. Sellon, Sea2c
William K. Shafer, F2c
Edward J. Shelden, FC1c
Eugene M. Skaggs, SM1c
Edward F. Slapikas, Sea1c
Merle A. Smith, EM3c
Walter H. Sollie, WT1c
Maurice V. Spangler, Sea1c
Ulis C. Steely, MM1c
Samuel C. Steiner, F1c
Everett R. Stewart, MM2c
Donald A. Stott, Sea1c
James Stouten, CBM (AA)
Charles H. Swanson, MM1c
Rangner F. Tanner, Jr., Sea2c
Houston Temples, Sea1c
Arthur R. Thinnes, Sea2c
Clarence Thompson, SC1c

Myron K. Lehman, Sea2c
Harold W. Lindsey, Sea2c
Alfred E. Livingston, F3c
Adolph J. Loebach, FC3c
Octavius Mabine, MAtt1c
Michael Malek, Sea2c
Walter B. Manning, EM1c
Joseph K. Maule, Sea1c
Donald R. McCloud, FC2c
Bert E. McKeeman, F1c
Lloyd E. McLaughlin, Sea2c
Herbert F. Melton, BM2c
Wallace G. Mitchell, Sea1c
John M. Mulick, HA1c
George E. Naegle, Sea1c
Paul A. Nash, FC1c
Arthur C. Neuenschwander, GM1c
Wilbur F. Newton, Sea1c
Harry E. Nichols, SK3c
Arnold M. Nielsen, BM1c
Joe R. Nightingale, Sea1c
Camillus M. O'Grady, Sea1c
Eli Olsen, SK3c
Lawrence J. Overley, FC2c
Millard C. Pace, F1c
Calvin H. Palmer, Sea2c
George L. Paradis, PhM3c
Dale F. Pearce, Sea2c
Stephen Pepe, WT1c
Wiley J. Perway, Bmkr2c
James N. Phipps, Sea2c
Rudolph V. Piskuran, Sea2c
Brady O. Prewitt, Sea2c
George F. Price, F1c
Jasper L. Pue, Jr., F3c
Eldon C. Ray, SK3c
Leo B. Regan, F1c
Porter L. Rich, WT2c
David J. Riley, Sea2c
Joseph M. Robertson, Sea2c
Walter B. Rogers, F1c
Charles L. Ruse, Mus2c
Roman W. Sadlowski, EM3c
Dean S. Sanders, CMM (PA)
Lyal J. Savage, Sea1c
Paul E. Saylor, F1c
Herman Schmidt, GM3c
Andrew J. Schmitz, F1c
Bernard O. Scott, MAtt1c
Verdi D. Sederstrom, Ens
Everett I. Severinson, SF1c
William J. Shanahan, Jr., SM3c
William G. Silva, GM1c
Garold L. Skiles, Sea2c
Leonard F. Smith, Msmth1c
Rowland H. Smith, Mus1c
James C. Solomon, Sea1c
Kirby R. Stapleton, Sea1c
Walter C. Stein, Sea1c
Charles M. Stern, Jr., Ens
Lewis S. Stockdate, Ens
Robert T. Stout, FC3c
Milton R. Surratt, Sea1c
Edward E. Talbert, Sea1c
Monroe Temple, Sea1c
Benjamin C. Terhune, F2c
Charles W. Thompson, F1c
George A. Thompson, Sea2c

Monument to USS *Tennessee* and USS *West Virginia*

Edward L. Conway, EM1c
Robert L. Corn, FFC1c
John W. Craig, SK1c
Samuel W. Crowder, F1c
Glenn G. Cyriack, SK2c
James W. Davenport, Jr., F1c
Leslie P. Delles, EM3c
Francis E. Dick, Mus2c
Kenneth E. Doernenburg, F1c
Carl D. Dorr, F2c
Stanislaw F. Drwall, Pmkr1c
Buford H. Dyer, Sea1c
Eugene K. Eberhardt, MM1c
Earl M. Ellis, RM3c
Julius Ellsberry, MAtt1c
Ignacio C. Farfan, MAtt1c
Lawrence H. Fecho, F1c
Robert A. Fields, EM3c
Francis C. Flaherty, Ens
Felicismo Florese, OS2c
George P. Foote, SK3c
Joy C. French, Sea2c
Michael Galajdik, F1c
Jesus F. Garcia, MAtt2c
Paul H. Gebser, MM1c
George T. George, Sea2c
George E. Giesa, F2c
George Gilbert, FC2c

Grant C. Cook, Jr., F1c
Beoin H. Corzatt, F1c
Warren H. Crim, F3c
William M. Curry, EM1c
Marshall E. Darby, Jr., Ens
Francis D. Day, CWT (PA)
Ralph A. Derrington, CMM (PA)
Leaman R. Dill, EM2c
John M. Donald, SF3c
Bernard V. Doyle, Sea2c
Cyril I. Dusset, MAtt1c
Wallace E. Eakes, SK3c
David B. Edmonston, Sea2c
Bruce H. Ellison, RM3c
John C. England, Ens
Luther J. Farmer, MM1c
Charlton H. Ferguson, Mus2c
William M. Finnegan, Ens
James M. Flanagan, Sea2c
Walter C. Foley, Sea1c
George C. Ford, F2c
Tedd M. Furr, CCM (AA)
Martin A. Gara, F2c
Eugene Garris, MAtt2c
Leonard R. Geller, F1c
George H. Gibson, EM3c
Quentin J. Gifford, RM2c
Warren C. Gillette, Sea1c

Harvey C. Herber, EM1c
Austin H. Hesler, SM3c
Joseph P. Hittorff, Jr., Ens
Herbert J. Hoard, CSK (PA)
Kenneth L. Holm, F3c
James W. Holzhauer, Sea1c
Chester G. Hord, SK3c
Charles E. Hudson, WT1c
Robert M. Hunter, Ens
Willie Jackson, OC1c
Challis R. James, Sea2c
Kenneth L. Jayne, F3c
Jesse B. Jenson, GM3c
Billy J. Johnson, F1c
Joseph M. Johnson, Sea1c
Charles A. Jones, Sea2c
Jerry Jones, MAtt3c
Wesley V. Jordan, Sea1c
Albert U. Kane, F1c
Howard V. Keffer, RM3c
Donald G. Keller, Sea1c
Warren J. Kempf, RM3c
William H. Kennedy, F1c
David L. Kesler, Bkr2c
Verne F. Knipp, Cox
William L. Kvidera, CM3cD.
Elliott D. Larsen, Mus1c
Elmer P. Lawrence, Sea1c

George Herbert, GM1c
Denis H. Hiskett, F1c
Frank S. Hoag, Jr., RM3c
Joseph W. Hoffman, Mus1c
Harry R. Holmes, F3c
Edwin C. Hopkins, F3c
Frank A. Hryniewicz, Sea1c
Lorentz E. Hultgren, MM2c
Claydon I. C. Iverson, F3c
Herbert B. Jacobson, F3c
George W. Jarding, F3c
Theodore Q. Jensen, RM3c
Charles H. Johannes, Sea2c
Edward D. Johnson, F1c
Jim H. Johnston, F1c
Fred M. Jones, MM1c
Julian B. Jordan, Lt.
Thomas V. Jurashen, Sea2c
John A. Karli, Sea1c
Ralph H. Keil, Sea1c
Joe M. Kelley, Sea2c
Leo T. Keninger, F1c
Elmer T. Kerestes, F1c
William A. Klasing, EM3c
Hans C. Kvalnes, Sea2c
T. Kyser, Sea2c
Johnnie C. Laurie, MAtt1c
Willard I. Lawson, F3c

Irvin A. R. Thompson, Ens
Richard J. Thomson, Sea2c
Robert L. Thrombley, Sea2c
Lloyd R. Timm, Sea2c
Dante S. Tini, RM3c
Everett C. Titterington, F1c
Natale I. Torti, Sea1c
Harold F. Trapp, FC2c
Shelby Treadway, GM3c
Victor P. Tumlinson, FC3c
Louis J. Tushla, F1c
Lowell E. Valley, F2c
Lewis L. Wagoner, Sea2c
Robert N. Walkowiak, F3c
Charles E. Walters, Sea2c
Edward Wasielewski, Sea1c
James C. Webb, F1c
Alfred F. Wells, MM1c
John D. Wheeler, F2c
Jack D. White, Sea1
Eugene W. Wicker, Sea1c
George J. Wilcox, Jr., Sea2c
James C. Williams, Sea1c
Bernard R. Wimmer, FC1c
Starring B. Winfield, RM3c
Frank Wood, Sea2c
Winfred O. Woods, MM1c
John L. Wortham, GM2c
Eldon P. Wyman, Ens
Robert V. Young, Sea1c
Thomas Zvansky, CSM (PA)

William M. Thompson, Ens
Cecil H. Thornton, Sea2c
David F. Tidball, Sea1c
Lewis F. Tindall, F1c
Henry G. Tipton, Sea1c
Neal K. Todd, F1c
Orval A. Tranbarger, Sea1c
William H. Trapp, EM3c
William D. Tucker, F1c
Billy Turner, Sea1c
Russell O. Ufford, Sea2c
Durrell Wade, AMM2c
Harry E. Walker, SK1c
Eugene A. Walpole, Sea2c
James R. Ward, Sea1c
Richard L. Watson, Sea1c
William E. Welch, Sea1c
Ernest R. West, Sea1c
Claude White, CWT (PA)
Alton W. Whitson, EM3c
Lloyd P. Wiegand, Mus2c
Albert I. Williams, Mus2c
Wilbur S. Williams, OS3c
Everett G. Windle, Sea2c
Rex E. Wise, F1c
Lawrence E. Woods, F1c
Creighton H. Workman, F1c
Paul R. Wright, CWT (PA)
Martin D. Young, F2c
Joseph J. Yurko, WT1c

USS Pennsylvania BB-38, Battleship

Robert E. Arnott, PhM2c
Charles Braga, Jr., Y2c
Frederick A. Browne, GM3c
James E. Craig, Lt. Comdr
Dancil J. McIntosh, Sea2c
James P. Owens, RM3c
Damian M. Portillo, SC1c
William H. Rice, GM3c
Payton L. Vanderpool, Jr., F2c

Henry E. Baker, Jr., Cox
Evan B. Brekken, Sea1c
Harold K. Comstock, Sea1c
Clarence F. Haase, Sea1c
Joseph A. Huhofski, RM3c
Joseph W. Pace, RM3c
Richard R. Rall, Lt. (jg) (MC)
Martin R. Slifer, GM1c
Claude B. Watson, Jr., Sea1c

USS Pruitt DM-22, Light Minelayer

George R. Keith, RM3c Killed on the Pennsylvania

USS Shaw DD-373, Destroyer

Frank J. Annunziato, Sea1c
Albert J. Bolen, F1c
Leon Egbert, MAtt2c
Joseph L. B. Gaudrault, Sea1c
Rodney W. Jones, Sea2c
Robert C. McQuade, Sea1c
Chester L. Parks, Sea1c
Robert A. Petz, Sea1c
Edward J. Quirk, F1c
Benjamin N. Russell, AS
Frank W. Stief, Jr., SC2c
James R. Westbrook, Sea1c

Anthony Bilyi, SC3c
Guy W. Carroll, QM2c
Fred Fugate, CCStd (PA)
Paul G. Gosnell, GM1c
John S. McAllen, Sea2c
Clyde C. Moore, RM2c
George A. Penuel, Jr., BM2c
Daniel P. Platschorre, Sea2c
John T. Rainbolt, F1c
Johnnie H. Spaeth, Sea2c
Palmer L. Taylor, MAtt1c
Clyde Williams, Sea1c

Earnest C. Porter, Jr., EM2c

USS Sicard DM-21, Light Minelayer

Warren P. Hickok, Sea2c Killed on the Pennsylvania

USS Tennessee BB-43, Battleship

Jesse L. Adams, Sea1c   Alfred W. Hudgell, BM1c

J. B. Delane Miller, Cox
Gerald O. Smith, SK1c

Eugene O. Roe, Sea1c

USS Tracy DM-19, Light Minelayer

John A. Bird, Sea1c
Laddie J. Zacek, Sea1c
All three were killed on the Pennsylvania

John W. Pence, RM3c

USS Utah AG-16, Target/Gunnery Training Ship

William D. Arbuckle, Sea2c
Rudolph P. Bielka, Lt. Comdr
John E. Black, Lt. (jg)
Pallas F. Brown, Sea2c
Feliciano T. Bugarin, OC2c (Killed by "friendly fire" aboard Argonne)
George V. Chestnutt, Jr., Sea2c
Joseph U. Conner, F1c
David L. Crossett, Sea1c
Leroy Dennis, Sea2c
William H. Dosser, Sea2c
Melvyn A. Gandre, QM1c
Charles N. Gregoire, Sea2c
Clifford D. Hill, Sea2c
David W. Jackson, Ens
William A. Juedes, SC2c
Eric T. Kampmeyer, GM3c
William H. Kent, Sea1c
John G. Little III, Lt. (jg)
William E. Marshall, Jr., Sea2c
Charles O. Michael, Lt. Comdr
Donald C. Norman, Sea2c
Edwin N. Odgaard, EM2c
Forrest H. Perry, SC3c
Walter H. Ponder, MM1c
Ralph E. Scott, Sea1c
George R. Smith, Matt1c
Joseph B. Sousley, Sea2c
Peter Tomich, CWT (PA)
Michael W. Villa, F3c
Glen A. White, F1c

Joseph Barta, F3c
Virgil C. Bigham, Sea1c
John T. Blackburn, F1c
William F. Brunner, F3c

Lloyd D. Clippard, Sea2c
John R. Crain, F1c
Billy R. Davis, F2c
Douglas R. Rieckhoff, SM1c
Vernon J. Eidsvig, Sea1c
Kenneth M. Gift, BM2c
Herold A. Harveson, Lt. (jg)
Emery L. Houde, Bkr2c
Leroy H. Jones, Sea1c
John L. Kaelin, Y3c
Joseph N. Karabon, F1c
George W. LaRue, GM3c
Kenneth L. Lynch, Sea2c
Rudolph M. Martinez, EM3c
Marvin E. Miller, Sea2c
Orris N. Norman, F2c
Elmer A. Parker, CSK (PA)
James W. Phillips, Sea1c
Frank E. Reed, SF3c
Henson T. Shouse, F1c
Robert D. Smith, Sea1c
Gerald V. Strinz, F3c
Elmer H. Ulrich, F3c
Vernard O. Wetrich, FC1c

USS Vestal AR-4, Repair Ship

Harold R. Arneberg, F3c
Lowell B. Jackson, Sea2c
Raymond J. Kerrigan, MM1c
William H. Reid, F1c

William Duane, CBM (PA)
Charles W. Jones, Msmth2c
Guy E. Long, Sea2c

USS West Virginia BB-48, Battleship

Welborn L. Ashby, F3c
William L. Barnett, F3c
Mervyn S. Bennion, Capt (CO)
Fred H. Boyer, F1c
Ennis E. Brooks, F1c
Riley M. Brown, F1c
William C. Campbell, Cox
Harold K. Costill, F3c
Charles E. Cottier, F1c
Eugene V. Downing, Sea2c
George S. Dunn, Jr., Sea2c
Clement E. Durr, Sea1c
Roland W. Edwards, F2c
Richard B. England, MM2c
Jose S. N. Flores, Matt2c
Gilbert R. Fox, F1c
Angelo M. Gabriele, F1c
Bibian B. Gonzales, Sea1c

Benjamin E. Bargerhuff, Jr., SF3c
Frank J. Bartek, Jr., F2c
Charlie V. Booton, Sea1c
George O. Branham, Mldr1c
Charles D. Brown, EM3c
John E. Burgess, Jr., Sea2c
William G. Christian, Bkr2c
Louis A. Costin, F1c
Howard D. Cromwell, CM2c
Donald L. Drum, F2c
Edward N. Durkee, CMM (AA)
Tommy Dye, F1c
Ronald B. Endicott, F3c
Woodrow W. Evans, GM3c
Jack Foth, EM1c
Neil D. Frye, Matt3c
Claude R. Garcia, SF2c
Myron E. Goodwin, Sea2c

Arthur Gould, RM3c
Hugh B. Harriss, HA1c
Fred A. Hilt, MM1c
Joseph E. Hood, F1c
Ira D. Hudson, F3c
Carl S. Johnson, Sea1c
Chester F. Kleist, Cox
William P. Kubinec, F2c
Thomas F. Leary, F1c
Eugene V. Lish, Mus1c
Donald W. Lynch, F1c
Charles M. Mann, Sea1c
Donald J. Mathison, FC3c
Thomas A. McClelland, Ens
Clarence W. McComas, Sea1c
John A. Meglis, F1c
Enrique C. Mendiola, Matt1c
Wallace A. Montgomery, MM2c
Albin J. Mrace, WT2c
Earl T. Nermoe, Sea1c
Emile S. Noce, EM2c
Clifford N. Olds, F1c
Walter J. Paciga, Sea2c
Andrew A. Pinko, EM3c
Roy W. Powers, SF2c
Albert Renner, F2c
Ernest C. Rose, SC1c
Theodore H. Saulsbury, OC2c
George W. Scott, SK2c
Ernest E. Speicher, EM2c
George E. Taber, MM2c
Keith W. Tipsword, MM1c
Joseph Vogelgesang, Jr., F2c
Bethel E. Walters, F1c
Clyde R. Wilson, Sea1c

Harry J. Halvorsen, F1c
Hadley I. Heavin, F2c
Howard D. Hodges, F1c
William D. Horton, Sea1c
William C. Jackson, EM3c
Sanford V. Kelley, Jr., GM3c
Milton J. Knight, Jr., F1c
Henry E. LaCrosse, Jr., SK3c
Joseph S. L. Lemire, Sea1c
Royle B. Luker, F3c
Arnold E. Lyon, GM3c
Jesus M. Mata, Matt1c
Luther K. McBee, Sea1c
Lawrence J. McCollom, MM2c
Quentin G. McKee, Sea2c
John R. Melton, Sea1c
Joe E. Mister, Matt1c
William F. Morris, F1c
Clair C. Myers, Sea1c
Paul E. Newton, Sea1c
Maurice M. O'Connor, MM1c
Arnold J. Owsley, Sea1c
James A. Paolucci, Sea2c
Jack A. Pitcher, Sea1c
George B. Reid, SF1c
Leonard C. Richter, MM1c
Glenn D. Sahl, F3c
Richard M. Schuon, Jr., Sea1c
Gordon E. Smith, SK2c
Otis D. Sterling, Matt1c
Ernie E. Tibbs, CMM (PA)
Albert P. VanderGoore, F1c
Thomas G. Wagner, Sea1c
Harold Wilbur, CM3c
Lester F. Zobeck, Sea1c

Ford Island

PATROL SQUADRON 21
Theodore W. Croft, AOM1c

Kaneohe Naval Air Station

HEADQUARTERS, NAVAL AIR STATION
Stanley D. Dosick, Sea1c

PATROL SQUADRON 11
John D. Buckley, AOM3c
Rodney S. Foss, Ens
James H. Robinson, Sea2c
Luther D. Weaver, Sea1c

Clarence M. Formoe, AMM1c
Milburn A. Manning, AMM3c
Joseph G. Smartt, Ens

PATROL SQUADRON 12
Walter S. Brown, AMM2c
Daniel T. Griffin, AMM1c
Charles Lawrence, AMM2c
Robert K. Porterfield, AMM3c
Raphael A. Watson, AMM1c

Lee Fox, Jr., Ens
George W. Ingram, Sea2c
Carl W. Otterstetter, Sea2c
Robert W. Uhlmann, Ens

PATROL SQUADRON 14
Laxton G. Newman, AMM3c

Pearl Harbor Naval Hospital

Arthur W. Russett, PhM1c

NAVAL MOBILE HOSPITAL #2
John H. Thuman, PhM3c

Hickam Field Memorial

USS Arizona BB-39, Battleship

1,177 sailors and marines died on the USS Arizona.

Name	Rank	Service
AARON, Hubert Charles Titus	F2c	USN
ABERCROMBIE, Samuel Adolphus	S1c	USN
ADAMS, Robert Franklin	S1c	USN
ADKISON, James Dillion	S1c	USN
AGUIRRE, Reyner Aceves	S2c	USN
AGUON, Gregorio San N.	MATT1c	USN
AHERN, Richard James	F1c	USN
ALBEROVSKY, Francis Severin	BMKR1c	USN
ALBRIGHT, Galen Winston	S1c	USN
ALEXANDER, Elvis Author	S2c	USN
ALLEN, Robert Lee	SF3c	USN
ALLEN, William Clayborn	EM1c	USN
ALLEN, William Lewis	SK2c	USNR
ALLEY, Jay Edgar	GM1c	USN
ALLISON, Andrew K.	F1c	USN
ALLISON, J. T.	F1c	USN
ALTEN, Ernest Mathew	S2c	USN
AMON, Frederick Purdy	S1c	USN
AMUNDSON, Leo DeVere	PVT	USMC
ANDERSON, Charles Titus	CM2c	USN
ANDERSON, Delbert Jake	BM2c	USN
ANDERSON, Donald William	SM3c	USN
ANDERSON, Harry	S1c	USN
ANDERSON, Howard Taisey	F1c	USN
ANDERSON, Irwin Corinthis	MATT1c	USN
ANDERSON, James Pickins Jr.	S1c	USN
ANDERSON, Lawrence Donald	ENS	USNR
ANDERSON, Robert Adair	GM3c	USN
ANDREWS, Brainerd Wells	CCMP	USN
ANGLE, Earnest Hersea	F2c	USN
ANTHONY, Glenn Samuel	S1c	USN
APLIN, James Raymond	CWTP	USN
APPLE, Robert William	F1c	USN
APREA, Frank Anthony	COX	USN
ARLEDGE, Eston	SM2c	USN
ARNAUD, Achilles	F3c	USN
ARNEBERG, William Robert	F2c	USN
ARNOLD, Claude Duran Jr.	F3c	USN

Name	Rank	Service
ARNOLD, Thell	SC1c	USN
ARRANT, John Anderson	MM1c	USN
ARVIDSON, Carl Harry	CMMP	USN
ASHMORE, Wilburn James	S2c	USN
ATCHISON, John Calvin	PVT	USMC
ATKINS, Gerald Arthur	HA1c	USN
AUSTIN, Laverne Alfred	S1c	USN
AUTRY, Eligah T. Jr.	COX	USN
AVES, Willard Charles	F2c	USN
AYDELL, Miller Xavier	WT2c	USN
AYERS, Dee Cumpie	S2c	USN
BADILLA, Manuel Domonic	F1c	USN
BAILEY, George Richmond	PFC	USMC
BAIRD, Billy Bryon	S1c	USN
BAJORIMS, Joseph	S1c	USN
BAKER, Robert Dewey	CMM	USN
BALL, William V.	S1c	USN
BANDY, Wayne Lynn	MUS2c	USN
BANGERT, John Henry	FC1c	USN
BARAGA, Joseph	SGT	USMC
BARDON, Charles Thomas	S2c	USN
BARKER, Loren Joe	COX	USN
BARNER, Walter Ray	S2c	USN
BARNES, Charles Edward	Y3c	USN
BARNES, Delmar Hayes	LTJG	USNR
BARNETT, William Thermon	S2c	USN
BARTLETT, David William	CPL	USMC
BARTLETT, Paul Clement	MM1c	USN
BATES, Edward Munroe Jr.	ENS	USNR
BATES, Tobert Alvin	PHM3c	USN
BATOR, Edward	F1c	USN
BAUER, Harold Walter	RM3c	USN
BEATON, Freddie	PVT	USMC
BEAUMONT, James Ammon	S2c	USN
BECK, George Richard	S1c	USN
BECKER, Marvin Otto	GM3c	USN
BECKER, Wesley Paulson	S1c	USN
BEDFORD, Purdy Renaker	F1c	USN
BEERMAN, Henry Carl	CM3c	USN
BEGGS, Harold Eugene	F1c	USN
BELL, Hershel Homer	FC2c	USN
BELL, Richard Leroy	S2c	USN
BELLAMY, James Curtis	OS3c	USN
BELT, Everett Ray Jr.	PFC	USMC

Name	Rank	Service
BENFORD, Sam Austin	BKR2c	USN
BENNETT, William Edmond Jr.	Y3c	USN
BENSON, James Thomas	S1c	USN
BERGIN, Roger Joseph	F2c	USN
BERKANSKI, Albert Charles	COX	USN
BERNARD, Frank Peter	F2c	USN
BERRY, Gordon Eugene	F2c	USN
BERRY, James Winford	F2c	USN
BERSCH, Arthur Anthony	S1c	USN
BERTIE, George Allan Jr.	S2c	USN
BIBBY, Charles Henry	F2c	USN
BICKEL, Kenneth Robert	F1c	USN
BICKNELL, Dale Deen	S1c	USN
BIRCHER, Frederick Robert	RM3c	USN
BIRDSELL, Rayon Delois	F2c	USN
BIRGE, George Albert	S1c	USN
BISHOP, Grover Barron	MM1c	USN
BISHOP, Millard Charles	F3c	USN
BISHOP, Wesley Horner Jr.	RM3c	USNR
BLACK, James Theron	PVT	USMC
BLAIS, Albert Edward	RM3c	USNR
BLAKE, James Monroe	F2c	USN
BLANCHARD, Albert Richard	COX	USN
BLANKENSHIP, Theron A.	S1c	USN
BLANTON, Atticus Lee	SF3c	USN
BLIEFFERT, Richmond Frederick	S1c	USN
BLOCK, Ivan Lee	PHM2c	USN
BLOUNT, Wayman Boney	S1c	USN
BOGGESS, Roy Eugene	SF2c	USN
BOHLENDER, Sam	GM2c	USN
BOLLING, Gerald Revese	S1c	USN
BOLLING, Walter Karr	F3c	USN
BOND, Burnis Leroy	CPL	USMC
BONEBRAKE, Buford Earl	F2c	USN
BONFIGLIO, William John	EM1c	USN
BOOTH, Robert Sinclair Jr.	ENS	USNR
BOOZE, Asbury Legare	BM1c	USN
BORGER, Richard	CMMA	USN
BOROVICH, Joseph John	S1c	USN
BORUSKY, Edwin Charles	CPL	USMC
BOSLEY, Kenneth Leroy	EM3c	USN
BOVIALL, Walter Robert	AMM2c	USN
BOWMAN, Howard Alton	S2c	USN
BOYD, Charles Andrew	CM3c	USN
BOYDSTUN, Don Jasper	S2c	USN
BOYDSTUN, R. L.	S2c	USN
BRABBZSON, Oran Merrill	MUS2c	USN
BRADLEY, Bruce Dean	S2c	USN
BRAKKE, Kenneth Gay	F3c	USN
BRICKLEY, Eugene	PVT	USMC
BRIDGES, James Leon	S1c	USN
BRIDGES, Paul Hyatt	S1c	USN
BRIDIE, Robert Maurice	F1c	USN
BRIGNOLE, Erminio Joseph	S2c	USN
BRITTAN, Charles Edward	S2c	USN
BROADHEAD, Johnnie Cecil	F2c	USN
BROCK, Walter Pershing	S1c	USN
BROMLEY, George Edward	SM3c	USN
BROMLEY, Jimmie	S1c	USN
BROOKS, Robert Neal	ENS	USNR
BROOME, Loy Raymond	SM3c	USN
BROONER, Allen Ottis	S1c	USN
BROPHY, Myron Alonzo	F2c	USN
BROWN, Charles Martin	S2c	USN
BROWN, Elwyn Leroy	EM3c	USN
BROWN, Frank George	QM3c	USN
BROWN, Richard Corbett	S1c	USN
BROWN, William Howard	S2c	USN

Name	Rank	Service
BROWNE, Harry Lamont	CMMA	USN
BROWNING, Tilmon David	S1c	USN
BRUNE, James William	RM3c	USNR
BRYAN, Leland Howard	S1c	USN
BRYANT, Lloyd Glenn	BM2c	USN
BUCKLEY, Jack C.	FC3c	USN
BUDD, Robert Emile	F2c	USN
BUHR, Clarence Edward	S1c	USN
BURDEN, Ralph Leon	RM3c	USN
BURDETTE, Ralph Warren	MUS2c	USN
BURKE, Frank Edmond Jr.	SK2c	USN
BURNETT, Charlie Leroy	S2c	USN
BURNS, John Edward	F1c	USN
BUSICK, Dewey Olney	F3c	USN
BUTCHER, David Adrian	F2c	USN
BUTLER, John Dabney	F1c	USN
BYRD, Charles Dewitt	S1c	USN
CADE, Richard Esh	S2c	USN
CALDWELL, Charles Jr.	F3c	USN
CALLAGHAN, James Thomas	BM2c	USN
CAMDEN, Raymond Edward	S2c	USN
CAMM, William Fielden	Y2c	USN
CAMPA, Ralph	S1c	USN
CAMPBELL, Burdette Charles	S1c	USN
CAPLINGER, Donald William	SC3c	USN
CAREY, Francis Lloyd	SK3c	USN
CARLISLE, Robert Wayne	S1c	USNR
CARLSON, Harry Ludwig	SK3c	USN
CARMACK, Harold Milton	F2c	USN
CARPENTER, Robert Nelson	MATT1c	USN
CARROLL, Robert Lewis	S1c	USN
CARTER, Burton Lowell	S2c	USN
CARTER, Paxton Turner	WO(PYCLK)	USN
CASEY, James Warren	S1c	USN
CASILAN, Epifanio Miranda	OS3c	USN
CASKEY, Clarence Merton	S1c	USN
CASTLEBERRY, Claude W. Jr.	S1c	USN
CATSOS, George	F1c	USN
CHACE, Raymond Vincent	CSKP	USN
CHADWICK, Charles Bruce	MM2c	USN
CHADWICK, Harold	MATT1c	USN
CHANDLER, Donald Ross	PVT	USMC
CHAPMAN, Naaman N.	S1c	USN
CHARLTON, Charles Nicholas	WT1c	USNR
CHERNUCHA, Harry Gregory	MUS2c	USN
CHESTER, Edward	S1c	USN
CHRISTENSEN, Elmer Emil	MM2c	USN
CHRISTENSEN, Lloyd Raymond	F1c	USN
CHRISTIANSEN, Edward Lee	BKR3c	USN
CIHLAR, Lawrence John	PHM3c	USN
CLARK, George Francis	GM3c	USN
CLARK, John Crawford Todd	F3c	USN
CLARK, Malcolm	BKR3c	USN
CLARK, Robert William Jr.	FC3c	USN
CLARKE, Robert Eugene	S1c	USN
CLASH, Donald	F2c	USN
CLAYTON, Robert Roland	COX	USN
CLEMMENS, Claude Albert	S1c	USN
CLIFT, Ray Emerson	COX	USN
CLOUES, Edward Blanchard	ENS	USN
CLOUGH, Edward Hay	GM1c	USN
COBB, Ballard Burgher	S1c	USN
COBURN, Walter Overton	S1c	USN
COCKRUM, Kenneth Earl	MM1c	USN
COFFIN, Robert	SF3c	USN
COFFMAN, Marshall Herman	GMec	USN
COLE, Charles Warren	SGT	USMC
COLE, David Lester	ENS	USNR

Name	Rate	Branch	Name	Rate	Branch	Name	Rate	Branch	Name	Rate	Branch
COLEGROVE, Willett S. Jr.	S2c	USN	DRIVER, Bill Lester	RM3c	USN	FLANNERY, James Lowell	SK3c	USN	HALLORAN, William Ignatius	ENS	USNR
COLLIER, John	F2c	USN	DUCREST, Louis Felix	S1c	USN	FLEETWOOD, Donald Eugene	PFC	USMC	HAMEL, Don Edgar	FLDMUS	USMCR
COLLIER, Linald Long Jr.	BKR3c	USN	DUKE, Robert Edward	CCSTDA	USN	FLOEGE, Frank Norman	MUS2c	USN	HAMILTON, Clarence James	MM1c	USN
COLLINS, Austin	SF3c	USN	DULLUM, Jerald Fraser	EM3c	USN	FLORY, Max Edward	S2c	USN	HAMILTON, Edwin Carrell	S1c	USN
COLLINS, Billy Murl	S1c	USN	DUNAWAY, Kenneth Leroy	EM3c	USN	FONES, George Everett	FC3c	USN	HAMILTON, William Holman	GM3c	USN
CONLIN, Bernard Eugene	S2c	USN	DUNHAM, Elmer Marvin	S1c	USN	FORD, Jack C.	S1c	USN	HAMMERUD, George Winston	S1c	USN
CONLIN, James Leo	F2c	USN	DUNNAM, Robert Wesley	PVT	USMCR	FORD, William Walker	EM3c	USN	HAMPTON, "J" "D"	F1c	USN
CONNELLY, Richard Earl	CQMA	USN	DUPREE, Arthur Joseph	F2c	USN	FOREMAN, Elmer Lee	F2c	USN	HAMPTON, Ted "W" Jr.	S1c	USN
CONRAD, Homer Milton Jr.	S1c	USN	DURHAM, William Teasdale	S1c	USN	FORTENBERRY, Alvie Charles	COX	USN	HAMPTON, Walter Lewis	BM2c	USN
CONRAD, Robert Frank	S2c	USN	DURIO, Russell	PFC	USMC	FOWLER, George Parten	S2c	USN	HANNA, David Darling	EM3c	USN
CONRAD, Walter Ralph	QM2c	USN	DUVEENE, John	1SGT	USMC	FOX, Daniel Russell	LTCOL	USMC	HANSEN, Carlyle B.	MM2c	USN
COOPER, Clarence Eugene	F2c	USN	DVORAK, Alvin Albert	BM2c	USN	FRANK, Leroy George	S1c	USN	HANSEN, Harvey Ralph	S1c	USN
COOPER, Kenneth Erven	F2c	USN	EATON, Emory Lowell	F3c	USN	FREDERICK, Charles Donald	EM2c	USN	HANZEL, Edward Joseph	WT1c	USN
CORCORAN, Gerard John	S1c	USN	EBEL, Walter Charles	CTCP	USN	FREE, Thomas Augusta	MM1c	USN	HARDIN, Charles Eugene	S1c	USN
COREY, Ernest Eugene	PHM3c	USN	EBERHART, Vincent Henry	COX	USN	FREE, William Thomas	S2c	USN	HARGRAVES, Kenneth William	S2c	USN
CORNELIUS, P. W.	SC3c	USN	ECHOLS, Charles Louis Jr.	EM3c	USN	FRENCH, John Edmund	LCDR	USN	HARMON, William D.	PFC	USMC
CORNING, Russell Dale	RM3c	USN	ECHTERNKAMP, Henry Clarence	S1c	USN	FRIZZELL, Robert Niven	S2c	USN	HARRINGTON, Keith Homer	S1c	USN
COULTER, Arthur Lee	S1c	USN	EDMUNDS, Bruce Roosevelt	Y2c	USN	FULTON, Robert Wilson	AMSMTH1c	USN	HARRIS, George Ellsworth	MM1c	USN
COWAN, William	COX	USN	EERNISSE, William Frederick	PTR1c	USN	FUNK, Frank Francis	BM2c	USN	HARRIS, Hiram Dennis	S1c	USN
COWDEN, Joel Beman	S2c	USN	EGNEW, Robert Ross	S1c	USN	FUNK, Lawrence Henry	S1c	USN	HARRIS, James William	F1c	USN
COX, Gerald Blinton	MUS2c	USN	EHLERT, Casper	SM3c	USN	GAGER, Roy Arthur	S2c	USN	HARRIS, Noble Burnice	COX	USN
COX, William Milford	S1c	USN	EHRMANTRAUT, Frank Jr.	S1c	USN	GARGARO, Ernest Russell	S2c	USN	HARRIS, Peter John	COX	USN
CRAFT, Harley Wade	CM3c	USN	ELLIS, Francis Arnold Jr.	EM3c	USN	GARLINGTON, Raymond Wesley	S1c	USN	HARTLEY, Alvin	GM3c	USN
CRAWLEY, Wallace Dewight	COX	USN	ELLIS, Richard Everett	S2c	USN	GARRETT, Orville Wilmer	SF2c	USN	HARTSOE, Max June	GM3c	USN
CREMEENS, Louis Edward	S1c	USN	ELLIS, Wilbur Danner	RM2c	USN	GARTIN, Gerald Ernest	S1c	USN	HARTSON, Lonnie Moss	SM3c	USN
CRISCUOLO, Michael	Y2c	USN	ELWELL, Royal	S1c	USN	GAUDETTE, William Frank	S1c	USN	HASL, James Thomas	F1c	USN
CRISWELL, Wilfred John	S1c	USN	EMBREY, Bill Eugene	F3c	USN	GAULTNEY, Ralph Martin	Em3c	USN	HAVERFIELD, James Wallace	ENS	USNR
CROWE, Cecil Thomas	GM2c	USN	EMERY, Jack Marvin	ENS	USN	GAZECKI, Philip Robert	ENS	USNR	HAVINS, Harvey Linfille	S1c	USN
CROWLEY, Thomas Ewing	LCDR(DC)	USN	EMERY, John Marvin	GM3c	USN	GEBHARDT, Kenneth Edward	S1c	USN	HAWKINS, Russell Dean	SM3c	USN
CURRY, William Joseph	WT2c	USN	EMERY, Wesley Vernon	SK2c	USN	GEER, Kenneth Floyd	S2c	USN	HAYES, John Doran	BM1c	USN
CURTIS, Lloyd B.	S1c	USN	ENGER, Stanley Gordon	GM3c	USN	GEISE, Marvin Frederick	S1c	USN	HAYES, Kenneth Merle	F1c	USN
CURTIS, Lyle Carl	RM2c	USN	ERICKSON, Robert	S1c	USN	GEMIENHARDT, Samuel Henry Jr.	MM2c	USN	HAYNES, Curtis James	QM2c	USN
CYBULSKI, Harold Bernard	S1c	USN	ERSKINE, Robert Charles	PFC	USMC	GHOLSTON, Roscoe	Y2c	USN	HAYS, William Henry	SK3c	USN
CYCHOSZ, Francis Anton	S1c	USN	ERWIN, Stanley Joe	MM1c	USN	GIBSON, Billy Edwin	S1c	USN	HAZDOVAC, Jack Claudius	S1c	USN
CZARNECKI, Stanley	F1c	USN	ERWIN, Walton Aluard	S1c	USN	GIESEN, Karl Anthony	Y2c	USN	HEAD, Frank Bernard	CYA	USN
CZEKAJSKI, Theophil	SM3c	USNR	ESTEP, Carl James	S1c	USN	GILL, Richard Eugene	S1c	USN	HEATER, Verrell Roy	S1c	USN
DAHLHEIMER, Richard Norbert	S1c	USN	ESTES, Carl Edwen	S1c	USN	GIOVENAZZO, Michael James	WT2c	USN	HEATH, Alfred Grant	S1c	USN
DANIEL, Lloyd Naxton	Y1c	USN	ESTES, Forrest Jesse	F1c	USN	GIVENS, Harold Reuben	Y3c	USN	HEBEL, Max June	SM3c	USNR
DANIK, Andrew Joseph	S2c	USN	ETCHASON, Leslie Edgar	S1c	USN	GOBBIN, Angelo	SC1c	USN	HECKENDORN, Warren Guy	S1c	USN
DARCH, Phillip Zane	S1c	USN	EULBERG, Richard Henry	FC2c	USN	GOFF, Wiley Coy	S2c	USN	HEDGER, Jess Laxton	S1c	USN
DAUGHERTY, Paul Eugene	Em3c	USN	EVANS, David Delton	PVT	USMC	GOMEZ, Edward Jr.	S1c	USN	HEDRICK, Paul Henry	BM1c	USN
DAVIS, John Quitman	S1c	USN	EVANS, Evan Frederick	ENS	USNR	GOOD, Leland	S2c	USN	HEELY, Leo Shinn	S2c	USN
DAVIS, Milton Henry	S1c	USN	EVANS, Mickey Edward	S1c	USN	GOODWIN, William Arthur	S2c	USN	HEIDT, Edward Joseph	F1c	USN
DAVIS, Murle Melvin	RM2c	USN	EVANS, Paul Anthony	S1c	USN	GORDON, Peter Charles Jr.	F1c	USN	HEIDT, Wesley John	MM2c	USN
DAVIS, Myrle Clarence	F3c	USNR	EVANS, William Orville	S2c	USN	GOSSELIN, Edward Webb	ENS	USNR	HELM, Merritt Cameron	S1c	USN
DAVIS, Thomas Ray	SF1c	USN	EWELL, Alfred Adam	WT1c	USN	GOSSELIN, Joseph Adjutor	RM1c	USN	HENDERSON, William Walter	S2c	USN
DAVIS, Virgil Denton	PVT	USMC	EYED, George	SK3c	USN	GOULD, Harry Lee	S1c	USN	HENDRICKSEN, Frank	F2c	USN
DAVIS, Walter Mindred	F2c	USN	FALLIS, Alvin E.	PHM2c	USN	GOVE, Rupert Clair	S1c	USN	HERRICK, Paul Edward	PVT	USMC
DAWSON, James Berkley	PVT	USMC	FANSLER, Edgar Arthur	S1c	USN	GRANGER, Raymond Edward	F3c	USN	HERRING, James Junior	SM3c	USN
DAY, William John	S2c	USN	FARMER, John Wilson	COX	USN	GRANT, Lawrence Everett	Y3c	USN	HERRIOTT, Robert Asher Jr.	S1c	USN
DE ARMOUN, Donald Edwin	GM3c	USN	FEGURGUR, Nicolas San Nicolas	MATT2c	USN	GRAY, Albert James	S1c	USN	HESS, Darrel Miller	FC1c	USN
DE CASTRO, Vicente	OS3c	USN	FESS, John Junior	F1c	USN	GRAY, Lawrence Moore	F1c	USN	HESSDORFER, Anthony Joseph	MM2c	USN
DEAN, Lyle Bernard	COX	USN	FIELDS, Bernard	RM3c	USNR	GRAY, William James Jr.	S1c	USN	HIBBARD, Robert Arnold	BKR2c	USN
DELONG, Frederick Eugene	CPL	USMC	FIELDS, Reliford	MATT2c	USN	GREEN, Glen Hubert	S1c	USN	HICKMAN, Arthur Lee	SM3c	USN
DERITIS, Russell Edwin	S1c	USN	FIFE, Ralph Elmer	S1c	USN	GREENFIELD, Carroll Gale	S1c	USN	HICKS, Elmer Orville	GM3c	USN
DEWITT, John James	COX	USN	FILKINS, George Arthur	COX	USN	GRIFFIN, Lawrence J.	PFC	USMC	HICKS, Ralph Dueard	PTR2c	USNR
DIAL, John Buchanan	S1c	USN	FINCHER, Allen Brady	ACK	USMC	GRIFFIN, Reese Olin	EM3c	USN	HILL, Bartley Talor	AOM3c	USN
DICK, Ralph R.	GM1c	USN	FINCHER, Dexter Wilson	SGT	USMC	GRIFFITHS, Robert Alfred	EM3c	USN	HILTON, Wilson Woodrow	GM1c	USN
DINE, John George	F2c	USN	FINLEY, Woodrow Wilson	PFC	USMC	GRISSINGER, Robert Beryle	S2c	USN	HINDMAN, Frank Weaver	S1c	USN
DINEEN, Robert Joseph	S1c	USN	FIRTH, Henry Amis	F3c	USN	GROSNICKLE, Warren Wilbert	EM2c	USN	HODGES, Garris Vada	F2c	USN
DOBEY, Milton Paul Jr.	S1c	USN	FISCHER, Leslie Henry	S1c	USN	GROSS, Milton Henry	CSKA	USN	HOELSCHER, Lester John	HA1c	USN
DOHERTY, George Walter	S2c	USN	FISHER, Delbert Ray	S1c	USN	GRUNDSTROM, Richard Gunner	S2c	USN	HOLLAND, Claude Herbert Jr.	S2c	USN
DOHERTY, John Albert	MM2c	USN	FISHER, James Anderson	MATT1c	USN	GURLEY, Jesse Herbert	SK3c	USN	HOLLENBACH, Paul Zepp	S1c	USN
DONOHUE, Ned Burton	F1c	USN	FISHER, Robert Ray	S2c	USN	HAAS, Curtis Junior	MUS2c	USN	HOLLIS, Ralph	LTJG	USNR
DORITY, John Monroe	S1c	USN	FISK, Charles Porter III	Y1c	USN	HADEN, Samuel William	COX	USN	HOLLOWELL, George Sanford	COX	USN
DOUGHERTY, Ralph McClearn	FC1c	USN	FITCH, Simon	MATT1c	USN	HAFFNER, Floyd Bates	F1c	USN	HOLMES, Lowell D.	F3c	USN
DOYLE, Wand B.	COX	USN	FITZGERALD, Kent Blake	PVT	USMC	HAINES, Robert Wesley	S2c	USN	HOLZWORTH, Walter	MGYSGT	USMC
DREESBACH, Herbert Allen	PFC	USMC	FITZSIMMONS, Eugene James	F3c	USN	HALL, John Rudolph	CBMP	USN	HOMER, Henry Vernon	S1c	USN

HOPE, Harold W. — PVT — USMC
HOPKINS, Homer David — S1c — USN
HORN, Melvin Freeland — F3c — USN
HORRELL, Harvey Howard — SM1c — USN
HORROCKS, James William — CGMP — USN
HOSLER, John Emmet — S1c — USN
HOUSE, Clem Raymond — CWTP — USN
HOUSEL, John James — SK1c — USN
HOWARD, Elmo — S1c — USN
HOWARD, Rolan George — GM3c — USN
HOWE, Darrell Robert — S2c — USN
HOWELL, Leroy — COX — USN
HUBBARD, Haywood Jr. — MATT2c — USN
HUDNALL, Robert Chilton — PFC — USMC
HUFF, Robert Glenn — PVT — USMC
HUFFMAN, Clyde Franklin — F1c — USN
HUGHES, Bernard Thomas — MUS2c — USN
HUGHES, Lewis Burton Jr. — S1c — USN
HUGHES, Marvin Austin — PVT — USMCR
HUGHEY, James Clynton — S1c — USN
HUIE, Doyne Conley — HA1c — USN
HULTMAN, Donald Standly — PFC — USMC
HUNTER, Robert Fredrick — S1c — USN
HUNTINGTON, Henry Louis — S2c — USN
HURD, Willard Hardy — MATT2c — USN
HURLEY, Wendell Ray — MUS2c — USN
HUVAL, Ivan Joseph — S1c — USN
HUX, Leslie Creade — PFC — USMC
HUYS, Arthur Albert — S1c — USN
HYDE, William Hughes — COX — USN
IAK, Joseph Claude — Y3c — USN
IBBOTSON, Howard Burt — F1c — USN
INGALLS, Richard Fitch — SC3c — USN
INGALLS, Theodore "A" — SC3c — USN
INGRAHAM, David Archie — FC3c — USN
ISHAM, Orville Adalbert — CGMA — USN
ISOM, Luther James — S1c — USN
IVERSEN, Earl Henry — S2c — USN
IVERSEN, Norman Kenneth — S2c — USN
IVEY, Charles Andrew Jr. — S2c — USN
JACKSON, David Paul Jr. — S1c — USN
JACKSON, Robert Woods — Y3c — USN
JAMES, John Burditt — S1c — USN
JANTE, Edwin Earl — Y3c — USN
JANZ, Clifford Thurston — LT — USN
JASTRZEMSKI, Edwin Charles — S1c — USN
JEANS, Victor Lawrence — WT2c — USN
JEFFRIES, Keith — COX — USN
JENKINS, Robert Henry Dawson — S2c — USN
JENSEN, Keith Marlow — EM3c — USN
JERRISON, Donald D. — CPL — USMC
JOHANN, Paul Frederick — GM3c — USN
JOHNSON, David Andrew Jr. — OC2c — USN
JOHNSON, Edmund Russell — MM1c — USN
JOHNSON, John Russell — RM3c — USN
JOHNSON, Samuel Earle — CDR(MC) — USN
JOHNSON, Sterling Conrad — COX — USN
JOLLEY, Berry Stanley — S2c — USNR
JONES, Daniel Pugh — S2c — USN
JONES, Edmon Ethmer — S1c — USN
JONES, Floyd Baxter — MATT2c — USN
JONES, Harry Cecil — S1c — USN
JONES, Henry Jr. — MATT1c — USN
JONES, Homer Lloyd — S1c — USN
JONES, Hugh Junior — S2c — USN
JONES, Leland — S1c — USN
JONES, Quincy Eugene — PFC — USMC
JONES, Thomas Raymond — ENS — USNR

JONES, Warren Allen — Y3c — USN
JONES, Willard Worth — S1c — USN
JONES, Woodrow Wilson — S2c — USN
JOYCE, Calvin Wilbur — F2c — USN
JUDD, Albert John — COX — USN
KAGARICE, Harold Lee — CSKA — USN
KAISER, Robert Oscar — F1c — USN
KALINOWSKI, Henry — PVT — USMCR
KATT, Eugene Louis — S2c — USN
KEEN, Billy Mack — PVT — USMC
KELLER, Paul Daniel — MLDR2c — USN
KELLEY, James Dennis — SF3c — USN
KELLOGG, Wilbur Leroy — F1c — USN
KELLY, Robert Lee — CEMA — USN
KENISTON, Donald Lee — S2c — USN
KENISTON, Kenneth Howard — F3c — USN
KENNARD, Kenneth Frank — GM3c — USN
KENNINGTON, Charles Cecil — S1c — USN
KENNINGTON, Milton Homer — S1c — USN
KENT, Thomas Jr. — S2c — USN
KIDD, Isaac Campbell — RADM — USN
KIEHN, Ronald William — MM2c — USN

Honoring those who died at Kaneohe Naval Air Station.

KIESELBACH, Charles Ermin — CM1c — USN
KING, Gordon Blane — S1c — USN
KING, Leander Cleaveland — S1c — USN
KING, Lewis Meyer — F1c — USN
KING, Robert Nicholas Jr. — ENS — USNR
KINNEY, Frederick William — MUS1c — USN
KINNEY, Gilbert Livingston — QM2c — USN
KIRCHHOFF, Wilbur Albert — S1c — USN
KIRKPATRICK, Thomas Larcy — CAPT(CHC) — USN
KLANN, Edward — SC1c — USN
KLINE, Robert Edwin — GM2c — USN
KLOPP, Francis Lawrence — GM3c — USN
KNIGHT, Robert Wagner — EM3c — USN
KNUBEL, William Jr. — S1c — USN
KOCH, Walter Ernest — S1c — USN
KOENEKAMP, Clarence D. — F1c — USN
KOEPPE, Herman Oliver — SC3c — USN
KOLAJAJCK, Brosig — S1c — USN
KONNICK, Albert Joseph — CM3c — USN
KOSEC, John Anthony — BM2c — USN
KOVAR, Robert — S1c — USN
KRAHN, James Albert — PFC — USMC
KRAMB, James Henry — S1c — USN
KRAMB, John David — MSMTH1c — USN
KRAMER, Robert Rudolph — GM2c — USN
KRAUSE, Fred Joseph — S1c — USN
KRISSMAN, Max Sam — S2c — USN

KRUGER, Richard Warren — QM2c — USN
KRUPPA, Adolph Louis — S1c — USN
KUKUK, Howard Helgi — S1c — USN
KULA, Stanley — SC3c — USN
KUSIE, Donald Joseph — RM3c — USN
LA FRANCEA, William Richard — S1c — USN
LA MAR, Ralph "B" — FC3c — USN
LA SALLE, Willard Dale — S1c — USN
LADERACH, Robert Paul — FC2c — USN
LAKE, John Ervin Jr. — WO(PYCLK) — USN
LAKIN, Donald Lapier — S1c — USN
LAKIN, Joseph Jordan — S1c — USN
LAMB, George Samuel — CSFA — USN
LANDMAN, Henry — AM2c — USN
LANDRY, James Joseph Jr. — BKR2c — USN
LANE, Edward Wallace — COX — USN
LANE, Mancel Curtis — S1c — USN
LANGE, Richard Charles — S1c — USN
LANGENWALTER, Orville J. — SK2c — USN
LANOUETTE, Henry John — COX — USN
LARSON, Leonard Carl — F3c — USN
LATTIN, Bleecker — RM3c — USN

LEE, Carroll Volney Jr. — S1c — USN
LEE, Henry Lloyd — S1c — USN
LEEDY, David Alonzo — FC2c — USN
LEGGETT, John Goldie — BM2c — USN
LEGROS, Joseph McNeil — S1c — USN
LEIGH, Malcolm Hedrick — GM3c — USN
LEIGHT, James Webster — S2c — USN
LEOPOLD, Robert Lawrence — ENS — USNR
LESMEISTER, Steve Louie — EM3c — USN
LEVAR, Frank — CWTP — USNR
LEWIS, Wayne Alman — CM3c — USN
LEWISON, Neil Stanley — FC3c — USN
LIGHTFOOT, Worth Ross — GM3c — USN
LINBO, Gordon Ellsworth — GM1c — USN
LINCOLN, John William — F1c — USN
LINDSAY, James E. — PFC — USMC
LINDSAY, James Mitchell — SF2c — USN
LINTON, George Edward — F2c — USN
LIPKE, Clarence William — F2c — USN
LIPPLE, John Anthony — SF1c — USN
LISENBY, Daniel Edward — S1c — USN
LIVERS, Raymond Edward — S1c — USN
LIVERS, Wayne Nicholas — F1c — USN
LOCK, Douglas A. — S1c — USN
LOHMAN, Earl Wynne — S1c — USN
LOMAX, Frank Stuart — ENS — USN
LOMIBAO, Marciano — OS1c — USN

LONG, Benjamin Franklin — CYP — USN
LOUNSBURY, Thomas William — S2c — USN
LOUSTANAU, Charles Bernard — S1c — USN
LOVELAND, Frank Crook — S2c — USN
LOVSHIN, William Joseph — PFC — USMC
LUCEY, Neil Jermiah — S1c — USN
LUNA, James Edward — S2c — USN
LUZIER, Ernest Burton — MM2c — USN
LYNCH, Emmett Isaac — MUS2c — USN
LYNCH, James Robert Jr. — GM3c — USN
LYNCH, William Joseph Jr. — S1c — USN
MADDOX, Raymond Dudley — CEMP — USN
MADRID, Arthur John — S2c — USN
MAFNAS, Francisco Reyes — MATT2c — USN
MAGEE, Gerald James — SK3c — USN
MALECKI, Frank Edward — CYP — USN
MALINOWSKI, John Stanley — SM3c — USNR
MALSON, Harry Lynn — SK3c — USN
MANION, Edward Paul — S2c — USN
MANLOVE, Arthur Cleon — WO(ELEC) — USN
MANN, William Edward — GM3c — USN
MANNING, Leroy — S2c — USN
MANSKE, Robert Francis — Y2c — USN
MARINICH, Steve Matt — COX — USN
MARIS, Elwood Henry — S1c — USN
MARLING, Joseph Henry — S2c — USN
MARLOW, Urban Herschel — COX — USN
MARSH, Benjamin Raymond Jr. — ENS — USNR
MARSH, William Arthur — S1c — USN
MARSHALL, Thomas Donald — S2c — USN
MARTIN, Hugh Lee — Y3c — USN
MARTIN, James Albert — BM1c — USN
MARTIN, James Orrwell — S2c — USN
MARTIN, Luster Lee — F3c — USN
MASON, Byron Dalley — S2c — USN
MASTEL, Clyde Harold — S2c — USN
MASTERS, Dayton Monroe — GM3c — USN
MASTERSON, Cleburne E. Carl — PHM1c — USN
MATHEIN, Harold Richard — BMKR2c — USN
MATHISON, Charles Harris — S1c — USN
MATNEY, Vernon Merferd — F1c — USN
MATTOX, James Durant — AM3c — USN
MAY, Louis Eugene — SC2c — USN
MAYBEE, George Frederick — RM2c — USNR
MAYFIELD, Lester Ellsworth — F1c — USN
MAYO, Rex Haywood — EM2c — USN
MEANS, Louis — MATT1c — USN
MEARES, John Morgan — S2c — USN
MENEFEE, James Austin — S1c — USN
MENO, Vicente Gogue — MATT2c — USN
MENZENSKI, Stanley Paul — COX — USN
MERRILL, Howard Deal — ENS — USN
MILES, Oscar Wright — S1c — USN
MILLER, Chester John — F2c — USN
MILLER, Doyle Allen — COX — USN
MILLER, Forrest Newton — CEMP — USN
MILLER, George Stanley — S1c — USN
MILLER, Jessie Zimmer — S1c — USN
MILLER, John David — S1c — USN
MILLER, William Oscar — SM3c — USN
MILLIGAN, Weldon Hawvey — S1c — USN
MIMS, Robert Lang — S1c — USN
MINEAR, Richard J. Jr. — PFC — USMC
MLINAR, Joseph — COX — USN
MOLPUS, Richard Preston — CMSMTHP — USN
MONROE, Donald — MATT2c — USN
MONTGOMERY, Robert E. — S2c — USN
MOODY, Robert Edward — S1c — USN

Name	Rate	Branch	Name	Rate	Branch	Name	Rate	Branch	Name	Rate	Branch
MOORE, Douglas Carlton	S1c	USN	OCHOSKI, Henry Francis	GM2c	USN	RAWHOUSER, Glen Donald	F3c	USN	SANDERSON, James Harvey	MUS2c	USN
MOORE, Fred Kenneth	S1c	USN	OFF, Virgil Simon	S1c	USN	RAWSON, Clyde Jackson	BM1c	USN	SANFORD, Thomas Steger	F3c	USN
MOORE, James Carlton	SF3c	USN	OGLE, Victor Willard	S2c	USN	RAY, Harry Joseph	BM2c	USN	SANTOS, Filomeno	OC2c	USN
MOORHOUSE, William Starks	MUS2c	USN	OGLESBY, Lonnie Harris	S2c	USN	REAVES, Casbie	S1c	USN	SATHER, William Ford	PMKR1c	USN
MOORMAN, Russell Lee	S2c	USN	OLIVER, Raymond Brown	S1c	USN	RECTOR, Clay Cooper	SK3c	USN	SAVAGE, Walter Samuel Jr.	ENS	USNR
MORGAN, Wayne	S1c	USN	OLSEN, Edward Kern	ENS	USNR	REECE, John Jeffris	S2c	USN	SAVIN, Tom	RM2c	USN
MORGAREIDGE, James Orries	F2c	USN	OLSON, Glen Martin	S2c	USN	REED, James Buchanan Jr.	SK1c	USN	SAVINSKI, Michael	S1c	USN
MORLEY, Eugene Elvis	F2c	USN	ORR, Dwight Jerome	S1c	USN	REED, Ray Ellison	S2c	USN	SCHDOWSKI, Joseph	S1c	USN
MORRIS, Owen Newton	S1c	USN	ORZECH, Stanislaus Joseph	S2c	USN	REGISTER, Paul James	LCDR	USN	SCHEUERLEIN, George Albert	GM3c	USN
MORRISON, Earl Leroy	S1c	USN	OSBORNE, Mervin Eugene	F1c	USN	REINHOLD, Rudolph Herbert	PVT	USMC	SCHILLER, Ernest	S2c	USN
MORSE, Edward Charles	S2c	USN	OSTRANDER, Leland Grimstead	PHM3c	USN	RESTIVO, Jack Martin	Y2c	USN	SCHLUND, Elmer Pershing	MM1c	USN
MORSE, Francis Jerome	BM1c	USN	OTT, Peter Dean	S1c	USN	REYNOLDS, Earl Arthur	S2c	USN	SCHMIDT Vernon Joseph	S1c	USN
MORSE, George Robert	S2c	USN	OWEN, Fredrick Halden	S2c	USN	REYNOLDS, Jack Franklyn	S1c	USN	SCHNEIDER, William Jacob	PFC	USMC
MORSE, Norman Roi	WT2c	USN	OWENS, Richard Allen	SK2c	USN	RHODES, Birb Richard	F2c	USN	SCHRANK, Harold Arthur	BKR1c	USN
MOSS, Tommy Lee	MATT2c	USN	OWSLEY, Thomas Lea	SC2c	USN	RHODES, Mark Alexander	S1c	USN	SCHROEDER, Henry	BM1c	USN
MOSTEK, Francis Clayton	PFC	USMC	PACE, Amos Paul	BM1c	USN	RICE, William Albert	S2c	USN	SCHUMAN, Herman Lincoln	SK1c	USN
MOULTON, Gordon Eddy	F1c	USN	PARKES, Harry Edward	BM1c	USN	RICH, Claude Edward	S1c	USN	SCHURR, John	EM2c	USN
MUNCY, Claude	MM2c	USN	PAROLI, Peter John	BKR3c	USN	RICHAR, Raymond Lyle	S1c	USN	SCILLEY, Harold Hugh	SF2c	USN
MURDOCK, Charles Luther	WT1c	USN	PATTERSON, Clarence Rankin	PFC	USMC	RICHARDSON, Warren John	COX	USN	SCOTT, A. J.	S2c	USN
MURDOCK, Melvin Elijah	WT2c	USN	PATTERSON, Harold Lemuel	S1c	USN	RICHISON, Fred Louis	GM3c	USN	SCOTT, Crawford Edward	PFC	USMC
MURPHY, James Joseph	S1c	USN	PATTERSON, Richard Jr.	SF3c	USN	RICHTER, Albert Wallace	COX	USN	SCOTT, George Harrison	PFC	USMC
MURPHY, James Palmer	F3c	USN	PAULMAND, Hilery	OS2c	USN	RICO, Guadalupe Augustine	S1c	USN	SCRUGGS, Jack Leo	MUS2c	USN
MURPHY, Jessie Huell	S1c	USN	PAVINI, Bruno	S1c	USN	RIDDEL, Eugene Edward	S1c	USN	SEAMAN, Russell Otto	F1c	USN
MURPHY, Thomas J. Jr.	SK1c	USN	PAWLOWSKI, Raymond Paul	S1c	USN	RIGANTI, Fred	SF3c	USN	SEELEY, William Eugene	S1c	USN
MYERS, James Gernie	SK1c	USN	PEARCE, Alonzo Jr.	S1c	USN	RIGGINS, Gerald Herald	S1c	USN	SEVIER, Charles Clifton	S1c	USN
McCARRENS, James Francis	CPL	USMC	PEARSON, Norman Cecil	S2c	USN	RIVERA, Francisco Unpingoo	MATT2c	USN	SHANNON, William Alfred	S1c	USN
McCARY, William Moore	S2c	USN	PEARSON, Robert Stanley	F3c	USN	ROBERTS, Dwight Fisk	F1c	USN	SHARBAUGH, Harry Robert	GM3c	USN
McCLAFFERTY, John Charles	BM2c	USN	PEAVEY, William Howard	QM2c	USN	ROBERTS, Kenneth Franklin	BM2c	USN	SHARON, Lewis Purdie	MM2c	USN
McCLUNG, Harvey Manford	ENS	USNR	PECKHAM, Howard William	F2c	USN	ROBERTS, McClellan Taylor	CPHMP	USN	SHAW, Clyde Donald	S1c	USN
McFADDIN, Lawrence James	Y2c	USN	PEDROTTI, Francis James	PVT	USMC	ROBERTS, Walter Scott Jr.	RM1c	USN	SHAW, Robert K.	MUS2c	USN
McGLASSON, Joe Otis	GM3c	USN	PEERY, Max Valdyne	S2c	USN	ROBERTS, Wilburn Carle	BKR3c	USN	SHEFFER, George Robert	S1c	USN
McGRADY, Samme Willie Genes	MATT1c	USN	PELESCHAK, Michael	S1c	USN	ROBERTS, William Francis	S2c	USN	SHERRILL, Warren Joseph	Y2c	USN
McGUIRE, Francis Raymond	SK2c	USN	PELTIER, John Arthur	EM3c	USN	ROBERTSON, Edgar Jr.	MATT3c	USN	SHERVEN, Richard Stanton	EM3c	USN
McHUGHES, John Breckenridge	CWTA	USN	PENTON, Howard Lee	S1c	USN	ROBERTSON, James Milton	MM1c	USN	SHIFFMAN, Harold Ely	RM3c	USN
McINTOSH, Harry George	S1c	USN	PERKINS, George Ernest	F1c	USN	ROBINSON, Harold Thomas	S2c	USN	SHILEY, Paul Eugene	S1c	USN
McKINNIE, Russell	MATT2c	USN	PETERSON, Albert H. Jr.	FC3c	USN	ROBINSON, James William	S2c	USN	SHIMER, Melvin Irvin	S1c	USN
McKOSKY, Michael Martin	S1c	USN	PETERSON, Elroy Vernon	FC2c	USN	ROBINSON, John James	EM1c	USN	SHIVE, Gordon Eshom	PFC	USMC
McPHERSON, John Blair	S1c	USN	PETERSON, Hardy Wilbur	FC3c	USN	ROBINSON, Robert Warren	PHM3c	USN	SHIVE, Malcolm Holman	RM3c	USNR
NAASZ, Erwin H.	SF2c	USN	PETERSON, Roscoe Earl	S2c	USN	ROBY, Raymond Arthur	S1c	USN	SHIVELY, Benjamin Franklin	F1c	USN
NADEL, Alexander Joseph	MUS2c	USN	PETTIT, Charles Ross	CRMP	USN	RODGERS, John Dayton	S1c	USN	SHORES, Irland Jr.	S1c	USN
NATIONS, James Garland	FC2c	USN	PETYAK, John Joseph	S1c	USN	ROEHM, Harry Turner	MM2c	USN	SHUGART, Marvin John	S1c	USN
NAYLOR, "J" "D"	SM2c	USN	PHELPS, George Edward	S1c	USN	ROGERS, Thomas Spurgeon	CWTP	USN	SIBLEY, Delmar Dale	S1c	USN
NEAL, Tom Dick	S1c	USN	PHILBIN, James Richard	S1c	USN	ROMANO, Simon	OC1c	USN	SIDDERS, Russell Lewis	S1c	USN
NECESSARY, Charles Raymond	S1c	USN	PIASECKI, Alexander Louis	CPL	USMC	ROMBALSKI, Donald Roger	S2c	USN	SIDELL, John Henry	GM2c	USN
NEIPP, Paul	S2c	USN	PIKE, Harvey Lee	EM3c	USN	ROMERO, Vladimir M.	S1c	USN	SILVEY, Jesse	MM2c	USN
NELSEN, George	SC2c	USN	PIKE, Lewis Jackson	S1c	USN	ROOT, Melvin Lenord	S1c	USN	SIMENSEN, Carleton Elliott	2LT	USMC
NELSON, Harl Coplin	S1c	USN	PINKHAM, Albert Wesley	S2c	USN	ROSE, Chester Clay	BM1c	USN	SIMON, Walter Hamilton	S1c	USN
NELSON, Henry Clarence	BM1c	USN	PITCHER, Walter Giles	GM1c	USN	ROSENBERY, Orval Robert	SF2c	USN	SIMPSON, Albert Eugene	S1c	USN
NELSON, Lawrence Adolphus	CTCP	USN	POOL, Elmer Leo	S1c	USN	ROSS, Deane Lundy	S2c	USN	SKEEN, Harvey Leroy	S2c	USN
NELSON, Richard Eugene	F3c	USN	POOLE, Ralph Ernest	S1c	USN	ROSS, William Fraser	GM3c	USN	SKILES, Charley Jackson Jr.	S2c	USN
NICHOLS, Alfred Rose	S1c	USN	POST, Darrell Albert	CMMA	USN	ROWE, Eugene Joseph	S1c	USN	SKILES, Eugene	S2c	USN
NICHOLS, Bethel Allan	S1c	USN	POVESKO, George	S1c	USN	ROWELL, Frank Malcom	S2c	USN	SLETTO, Earl Clifton	MM1c	USN
NICHOLS, Clifford Leroy	TC1c	USN	POWELL, Jack Speed	PFC	USMC	ROYALS, William Nicholas	F1c	USN	SMALLEY, Jack G.	S1c	USN
NICHOLS, Louis Duffie	S2c	USN	POWELL, Thomas George	S1c	USN	ROYER, Howard Dale	GM3c	USN	SMART, George David	COX	USN
NICHOLSON, Glen Eldon	EM3c	USN	POWER, Abner Franklin	PVT	USMC	ROZAR, John Frank	WT2c	USN	SMESTAD, Halge Hojem	RM2c	USN
NICHOLSON, Hancel Grant	S1c	USN	PRESSON, Wayne Harold	S1c	USN	ROZMUS, Joseph Stanley	S1c	USN	SMITH, Albert Joseph	LTJG	USN
NIDES, Thomas James	EM1c	USN	PRICE, Arland Earl	RM2c	USN	RUDDOCK, Cecil Roy	S1c	USN	SMITH, Earl Jr.	S1c	USN
NIELSEN, Floyd Theadore	CM3c	USN	PRITCHETT, Robert Leo Jr.	S1c	USN	RUGGERIO, William	FC3c	USN	SMITH, Earl Walter	FC3c	USN
NOLATUBBY, Henry Ellis	PFC	USMC	PUCKETT, Edwin Lester	SK3c	USN	RUNCKEL, Robert Gleason	BUG1c	USN	SMITH, Edward	GM3c	USN
NOONAN, Robert Harold	S1c	USN	PUGH, John Jr.	SF3c	USN	RUNIAK, Nicholas	S1c	USN	SMITH, Harry	S2c	USNR
NOWOSACKI, Theodore Lucian	ENS	USNR	PUTNAM, Avis Boyd	SC3c	USN	RUSH, Richard Perry	S1c	USN	SMITH, John A.	SF3c	USN
NUSSER, Raymond Alfred	GM3c	USN	PUZIO, Edward	S1c	USN	RUSHER, Orville Lester	MM1c	USN	SMITH, John Edward	S1c	USN
NYE, Frank Erskine	S1c	USN	QUARTO, Mike Joseph	S1c	USN	RUSKEY, Joseph John	CBMP	USN	SMITH, Luther Kent	S1c	USN
O'BRIEN, Joseph Bernard	PFC	USMC	QUINATA, Jose Sanchez	MATT2c	USN	RUTKOWSKI, John Peter	S1c	USN	SMITH, Mack Lawrence	S1c	USN
O'BRYAN, George David	FC3c	USN	RADFORD, Neal Jason	MUS2c	USN	RUTTAN, Dale Andrew	EM3c	USN	SMITH, Marvin Ray	S1c	USN
O'BRYAN, Joseph Benjamin	FC3c	USN	RASMUSSEN, Arthur Severin	CM1c	USN	SAMPSON, Sherley Rolland	RM3c	USN	SMITH, Orville Stanley	ENS	USN
O'NEALL, Rex Eugene	S1c	USN	RASMUSSON, George Vernon	F3c	USN	SANDALL, Merrill Deith	SF3c	USN	SMITH, Walter Tharnel	MATT2c	USN
O'NEILL, William Thomas Jr.	ENS	USNR	RATKOVICH, William	WT1c	USN	SANDERS, Eugene Thomas	ENS	USN	SNIFF, Jack Bertrand	CPL	USMC

SOENS, Harold Mathias	SC1c	USN
SOOTER, James Fredrick	RM3c	USN
SORENSEN, Holger Earl	S1c	USN
SOUTH, Charles Braxton	S1c	USN
SPENCE, Merle Joe	S1c	USN
SPOTZ, Maurice Edwin	F1c	USN
SPREEMAN, Robert Lawrence	GM3c	USN
SPRINGER, Charles Harold	S2c	USN
STALLINGS, Kermit Braxton	F1c	USN
STARKOVICH, Charles	EM3c	USN
STARKOVICH, Joseph Jr.	F2c	USN
STAUDT, Alfred Parker	F3c	USN
STEFFAN, Joseph Philip	BM2c	USN
STEIGLEDER, Lester Leroy	COX	USN
STEINHOFF, Lloyd Delroy	S1c	USN
STEPHENS, Woodrow Wilson	EM1c	USN
STEPHENSON, Hugh Donald	S1c	USN
STEVENS, Jack Hazelip	S1c	USN
STEVENS, Theodore R.	AMM2c	USN
STEVENSON, Frank Jake	PFC	USMC
STEWART, Thomas Lester	SC3c	USN
STILLINGS, Gerald Fay	F2c	USN
STOCKMAN, Harold William	FC3c	USN
STOCKTON, Louis Alton	S2c	USN
STODDARD, William Edison	S1c	USN
STOPYRA, Julian John	RM3c	USN
STORM, Laun Lee	Y1c	USN
STOVALL, Richard Patt	PFC	USMC
STRANGE, Charles Orval	F2c	USN
STRATTON, John Raymond	S1c	USN
SUGGS, William Alfred	S1c	USN
SULSER, Frederick Franklin	GM3c	USN
SUMMERS, Glen Allen	Y1c	USN
SUMMERS, Harold Edgar	SM2c	USN
SUMNER, Oren	S2c	USN
SUTTON, Clyde Westly	CCSTDP	USN
SUTTON, George Woodrow	SK1c	USN
SWIONTEK, Stanley Stephen	FLDCK	USN
SWISHER, Charles Elijah	S1c	USN
SYMONETTE, Henry	OC1c	USN
SZABO, Theodore Stephen	PVT	USMCR
TAMBOLLEO, Victor Charles	SF3c	USN
TANNER, Russell Allen	GM3c	USN
TAPIE, Edward Casamiro	MM2c	USN
TAPP, Lambert Ray	GM3c	USN
TARG, John	CWTP	USN
TAYLOR, Aaron Gust	MATT1c	USN
TAYLOR, Charles Benton	EM3c	USN
TAYLOR, Harry Theodore	GM2c	USN
TAYLOR, Robert Denzil	COX	USN
TEELING, Charles Madison	CPRTP	USNR
TEER, Allen Ray	EM1c	USN
TENNELL, Raymond Clifford	S1c	USN
TERRELL, John Raymond	F2c	USN
THEILLER, Rudolph	S1c	USN
THOMAS, Houston O'Neal	COX	USN
THOMAS, Randall James	S1c	USN
THOMAS, Stanley Horace	F3c	USN
THOMAS, Vincent Duron	COX	USN
THOMPSON, Charles Leroy	S1c	USN
THOMPSON, Irven Edgar	S1c	USN
THOMPSON, Robert Gary	SC1c	USN
THORMAN, John Christopher	EM2c	USN
THORNTON, George Hayward	GM3c	USN
TINER, Robert Reaves	F2c	USN
TISDALE, William Esley	CWTP	USN
TRIPLETT, Thomas Edgar	S1c	USN
TROVATO, Tom	S1c	USN

TUCKER, Raymond Edward	COX	USN
TUNTLAND, Earl Eugene	S1c	USN
TURNIPSEED, John Morgan	F3c	USN
TUSSEY, Lloyd Harold	EM3c	USN
TYSON, Robert	FC3c	USN
UHRENHOLDT, Andrew Curtis	ENS	USNR
VALENTE, Richard Dominic	GM3c	USN
VAN ATTA, Garland Wade	MM1c	USN
VAN HORN, James Randolf	S2c	USN
VAN VALKENBURGH, Franklin	CAPT(CO)	USN
VARCHOL, Brinley	GM2c	USN
VAUGHAN, William Frank	PHM2c	USN
VEEDER, Gordon Elliott	S2c	USN
VELIA, Galen Steve	SM3c	USN
VIEIRA, Alvaro Everett	S2c	USN
VOJTA, Walter Arnold	S1c	USN
VOSTI, Anthony August	GM3c	USN
WAGNER, Mearl James	SC2c	USN
WAINWRIGHT, Silas Alonzo	PHM1c	USN
WAIT, Wayland Lemoyne	S1c	USN
WALKER, Bill	S1c	USN
WALLACE, Houston Oliver	WT1c	USN
WALLACE, James Frank	S1c	USN
WALLACE, Ralph Leroy	F3c	USN
WALLENSTIEN, Richard Henry	S1c	USN
WALTERS, Clarence Arthur	S2c	USN
WALTERS, William Spurgeon Jr.	FC3c	USN
WALTHER, Edward Alfred	FC3c	USN
WALTON, Alva Dowding	Y3c	USN
WARD, Albert Lewis	S1c	USN
WARD, William E.	COX	USN
WATKINS, Lenvil Leo	F2c	USN
WATSON, William Lafayette	F3c	USN
WATTS, Sherman Maurice	HA1c	USN
WATTS, Victor Ed	GM3c	USN
WEAVER, Richard Walter	S1c	USN
WEBB, Carl Edward	PFC	USMC
WEBSTER, Harold Dwayne	S2c	USN
WEEDEN, Carl Alfred	ENS	USN
WEIDELL, William Peter	S2c	USN
WEIER, Bernard Arthur	PVT	USMC
WELLER, Ludwig Fredrick	CSKP	USN
WELLS, Floyd Arthur	RM2c	USN
WELLS, Harvey Anthony	SF2c	USN
WELLS, Raymond Virgil Jr.	S1c	USN
WELLS, William Bennett	S1c	USN
WEST, Broadus Franklin	S1c	USN
WEST, Webster Paul	S1c	USN
WESTCOTT, William Percy Jr.	S1c	USN
WESTERFIELD, Ivan Ayers	S1c	USN
WESTIN, Donald Vern	F3c	USN
WESTLUND, Fred Edwin	BM2c	USN
WHISLER, Gilbert Henry	PFC	USMC
WHITAKER, John William Jr.	S1c	USN
WHITCOMB, Cecil Eugene	EM3c	USN
WHITE, Charles William	MUS2c	USN
WHITE, James Clifton	F1c	USN
WHITE, Vernon Russell	S1c	USN
WHITE, Volmer Down	S1c	USN
WHITEHEAD, Ulmont Irving Jr.	ENS	USN
WHITLOCK, Paul Morgan	S2c	USN
WHITSON, Ernest Hubert Jr.	MUS2c	USN
WHITT, William Byron	GM3c	USN
WHITTEMORE, Andrew Tiny	MATT2c	USN
WICK, Everett Morris	FC3c	USN
WICKLUND, John Joseph	S1c	USN
WILCOX, Arnold Alfred	QM2c	USN
WILL, Joseph William	S2c	USN

WILLETTE, Laddie James	S2c	USN
WILLIAMS, Adrian Delton	S1c	USN
WILLIAMS, Clyde Richard	MUS2c	USN
WILLIAMS, George	S1c	USN
WILLIAMS, Jack Herman	RM3c	USN
WILLIAMS, Laurence "A"	ENS(AV)	USNR
WILLIAMSON, Randolph Jr.	MATT2c	USN
WILLIAMSON, William Dean	RM2c	USNR
WILLIS, Robert Kenneth Jr.	S1c	USN
WILSON, Bernard Martin	RM3c	USN
WILSON, Comer A.	CBMP	USN
WILSON, Hurschel Woodrow	F2c	USN
WILSON, John James	S1c	USN
WILSON, Neil Mataweny	CWO(MACH)	USN
WILSON, Ray Milo	RM3c	USNR
WIMBERLY, Paul Edwin	GM3c	USN
WINDISH, Robert James	PVT	USMC
WINDLE, Robert England	PFC	USMC
WINTER, Edward	WO(MACH)	USNR
WITTENBERG, Russell Duane	PVT	USMC
WOJTKIEWICZ, Frank Peter	CMMP	USN
WOLF, George Alexanderson Jr.	ENS	USNR
WOOD, Harold Baker	BM2c	USN
WOOD, Horace Van	S1c	USN
WOOD, Roy Eugene	F1c	USN
WOODS, Vernon Wesley	S1c	USN
WOODS, William Anthony	S2c	USN
WOODWARD, Ardenne Allen	MM2c	USN
WOODY, Harlan Fred	S2c	USN
WOOLF, Norman Bragg	CWTP	USN
WRIGHT, Edward Henry	S2c	USN
WYCKOFF, Robert Leroy	F1c	USN
YATES, Elmer Elias	SC3c	USN
YEATS, Charles Jr.	COX	USN
YOMINE, Frank Peter	F2c	USN
YOUNG, Eric Reed	ENS	USN
YOUNG, Glendale Rex	S1c	USN
YOUNG, Jay Wesley	S1c	USN
YOUNG, Vivan Louis	WT1c	USN
ZEILER, John Virgel	S1c	USN
ZIEMBRICKE, Steve A.	S1c	USN
ZIMMERMAN, Fred	Cox	USN
ZIMMERMAN, Lloyd McDonald	S2c	USN
ZWARUN, Jr. Michael	S1c(S2c)	USN

Medal of Honor Recipients

☸

The following is a list of the recipients of the Congressional Medal of Honor.

*Captain Mervyn S. Bennion, USN
Aviation Chief Ordnanceman John W. Finn, USN
*Ensign Frank C. Flaherty, USNR
Lieutenant Commander Samuel G. Fuqua, USN
*Chief Boatswain Edwin J. Hill, USN
*Ensign Herbert C. Jones, USNR
*Rear Admiral Isaac C. Kidd, USN
Gunner Jackson C. Pharris, USN
*Chief Radioman Thomas J. Reeves, USN
Machinist Donald K. Ross, USN
*Machinist's Mate First Class Robert R. Scott, USN
*Chief Watertender Peter Tomich, USN
*Captain Franklin Van Valkenburgh, USN
*Seaman First Class James R. Ward, USN
Commander Cassin Young, USN

posthumous award

JAPANESE FORCES

●

Mobile Force

Akagi

Hajime Goto, PO1c	Takashi Hirano, PO1c
Kanesuke Honma, PO3c	Hirokichi Kinoshita, PO2c
Yoshikazu Ota, PO2c	Toshio Oyama, WO
Kiyoshi Sakamoto, PO2c	Chuji Shimakura, Sea1c
Shigeharu Sugaya, PO2c	Michikazu Utsuki, PO2c

Kaga

Nagaaki Asahi, PO3c	Ippei Goto, WO
Toru Haneda, PO2c	Fumio Hirashima, PO2c
Tomio Ienaga, PO1c	Fukumitsu Imai, PO1c
Naritoku Kikura, PO3c	Kazumi Kitahara, Sea1c
Kenichi Kumamoto, PO2c	Kazuyoshi Kuwahata, PO1c
Zenharu Machimoto, PO2c	Saburo Makino, Lt
Kichizo Masuda, PO2c	Isamu Matsuda, PO2c
Tokio Minasaki, PO3c	Tokinori Morita, WO
Kiyoshi Nagai, PO2c	Narikatsu Ohashi, Sea1c
Iwao Oka, Sea1c	Toshio Onishi, PO2c
Noboru Sakaguchi, PO3c	Toshiaki Sakato, PO3c
Seinoshin Sano, PO2c	Yoshio Shimizu, Sea1c
Sueo Sugita, WO	Mimori Suzuki, Lt
Fusatomi Takeda, PO2c	Tomoji Takeda, PO2c
Nobuo Tsuda, PO2c	Yonetaro Ueda, PO1c
Hisao Umezu, PO2c	

Hiryu

Isamu Kiyomura, PO2c	Hajime Murao, Sea1c
Shigenori Nishikaichi, PO1c	Yoshiiku Shimizu, PO2c
Tsunayoshi Toyama, PO2c	

Shokaku

Kunio Iwatsuki, Sea1c	Tetsuro Kumakura, Sea1c

Soryu

Takashi Atsumi, PO1c	Fusata Iida, Lt
Saburo Ishii, PO2c	Satoru Kawasaki, PO3c
Hideyasu Kuwahara, PO2c	Kenji Maruyama, PO3c
Ryoichi Takahashi, PO1c	

First Submarine Division
(Special Attack Unit)

I-16

Masaharu Yokoyama, Lt (jg)	Sadamu Ueda, PO2c

I-18

Shigemi Furuno, Lt (jg)	Shigenori Yokoyama, PO1c

I-20

Akira Hiro-o, Ensign	Yoshio Katayama, PO2c

I-22

Naoji Iwasa, Lt	Naokichi Sasaki, PO1c

I-24

Kiyoshi Inagaki, PO2c	

Bibliography

✪

Agawa, Hiroyuki. *The Reluctant Admiral: Yamamoto and the Imperial Navy*. Tokyo: Kodansha International, 1979.

Arian, Frank B. and Martin S. Jacobs. *Remember Pearl Harbor Collectibles*. Missoula, Montana: Pictorial Histories Publishing Company Inc., 2000.

Barnhart, Michael A. *Japan Prepares for Total War: The Search for Economic Security, 1919-1941*. Ithaca, NY: Cornell University Press, 1987.

Beach, Edward L. *Scapegoats: A Defense of Kimmel and Short at Pearl Harbor*. Annapolis, MD: Naval Institute Press, 1995.

Beasley, W.G. *The Japanese Experience*. London: Weidenfeld & Nicolson, 1999.

Behr, Edward. *Hirohito: Behind the Myth*. New York: Villard Books, 1989.

Brinkley, David. *Washington Goes to War*. New York: Ballantine, 1988.

Budiansky, Stephen. *Battle of Wits: The Complete Story of Codebreaking in World War II*. New York: The Free Press, 2000.

_____."Too Late for Pearl Harbor." An article in United States Naval Institute Proceedings, December 1999, Vol 125/12.

Burlingame, Burl. *Advance Force Pearl Harbor*. Kailua, Hawaii: Pacific Monograph, 1992.

Calvocoressi, Peter, Guy Wint and John Pritchard. *Total War: The Causes and Courses of the Second World War*. London: Viking, 1989.

Cohen, Stan. *East Wind Rain: A Pictorial History of the Pearl Harbor Attack*. Missoula, Montana: Pictorial Histories, 1999.

Costello, John. *The Pacific War*. London: Collins, 1981.

Deacon, Richard. *The Silent War: A History of Western Naval Intelligence*. London: Grafton, 1988.

Defense, US Department of. *The "Magic" Background of Pearl Harbor*. (Washington, DC: eight volumes, 1977.)

Dull, Paul. *A Battle History of the Imperial Japanese Navy*. Annapolis, MD: US Naval Institute Press, 1978.

Evans, David C. and Mark R. Peattie. *Kaigun: Strategy Tactics and Technology in the Imperial Japanese Navy, 1887-1941*. Annapolis, MD: Naval Institute Press, 1997.

Elphick, Peter. *Far Eastern File: The Intelligence War in the Far East 1930-1945*. London: Hodder & Stoughton, 1997.

Gallagher, Tad. *John Ford: The Man and his Films*. Berkeley: University of California Press, 1986.

Goldstein, Donald M. and Katherine V. Dillon (eds.). *The Pearl Harbor Papers: Inside the Japanese Plans*. New York: Brassey's (US), 1993.

Goldstein, Donald M., Katherine V. Dillon and J. Michael Wenger. *The Way It Was: Pearl Harbor, the Original Photographs*. New York: Brassey's (US), 1991.

Hattori, Takushiro. *The Complete History of the Greater East Asia War*. (English translation, Library of Congress, shelf 49330)

Honan, William H. Bywater. *The Man who Invented the Pacific War*. London: Macdonald, 1990.

Ienaga, Saburo. *Japan's Last War: World War II and the Japanese, 1931-1945*. Oxford: Blackwell, 1979.

Ike, Nobutaka (ed.). *Japan's Decision for War: Records of the 1941 Policy Conferences*. Stanford, CA: Stanford University Press, 1967.

Iriye, Akira. *Power and Culture: The Japanese-American War 1941-1945*. Cambridge, MA: Harvard University Press, 1981.

Jane's Publishing Co, London: *Fighting Ships of World War II*. (Reissued by Military Press, New York, 1989.)

Jones, James. *From Here to Eternity*. New York: Charles Scribner and Sons, 1951.

Kimball, Warren F. (ed.). *Churchill & Roosevelt: The Complete Correspondence* (three volumes). Princeton, NJ: Princeton University Press, 1984.

Kimmett, Larry and Margaret Regis. *The Attack on Pearl Harbor: An Illustrated History*. Seattle, WA: Navigator Publishing, 1999.

Layton, Edwin T., Roger Pineau and John Costello. *And I was There. Pearl Harbor and Midway: Breaking the Secrets*. New York: Morrow, 1985.

Lewin, Ronald. *The Other Ultra: Codes, Ciphers and the Defeat of Japan*. London: Hutchinson, 1982.

Lord, Walter. *Day of Infamy*. New York: Holt, 1957.

Love, Robert W. Jr. (ed.) *Pearl Harbor Revisited*. New York: St. Martin's Press, 1995.

Mason, Theodore C. *Battleship Sailor*. Annapolis, MD: Naval Institute Press, 1982.

Mason, John T. (ed.). *The Pacific War Remembered: An Oral History Collection*. Annapolis, MD: US Naval Institute Press, 1986.

McCain, John and Mark Slater. *Faith of My Fathers*. New York: Random House, 1999.

Miller, Edward S. *War Plan Orange*. Annapolis, MD: Naval Institute Press, 1991.

Morgan, Ted. *FDR: A Biography*. London: Grafton, 1987.

Morison, Rear Admiral Samuel Eliot, USNR. *History of the US Naval Operations in World War II* (15 volumes). Boston, MA: Little Brown, from 1947.

Okuyima, Masatake, Jiro Horikoshi and Martin Caidin. *Zero: The Story of the Japanese Navy Air Force*. London: Cassell, 1957.

Prados, John. *Combined Fleet Decoded: The Secret History of American Intelligence and the Japanese Navy in World War II*. New York: Random House, 1995.

Prange, Gordon W. *At Dawn We Slept: The Untold Story of Pearl Harbor* (revised ed.). New York: Penguin, 1991.

Rusbridger, James and Eric Nave. *Betrayal at Pearl Harbor*. New York: Summit Books, 1991.

Sakamaki, Kazuo. *I Attacked Pearl Harbor*. New York: Association Press, 1949.

Simpson, B. Mitchell. *Admiral Harold R. Stark, Architect of Victory, 1939-45*. Charleston, SC: University of South Carolina Press, 1989.

Smith, Michael. *The Emperor's Codes*. London: Bantam, 2000.

Spector, Ronald H. *Eagle Against the Sun*. London: Penguin, 1987.

Stillwell, Paul. *Air Raid, Pearl Harbor!: Recollections of a Day of Infamy*. Annapolis, MD: Naval Institute Press, 1981.

_____. *Battleship Arizona*. Annapolis, MD: Naval Institute Press, 1991.

Stinnett, Robert B. *Day of Deceit: The Truth about FDR and Pearl Harbor*. London: Constable, 2000.

Terkel, Studs. *The Good War*. London: Penguin, 1986.

Toland, John. *Infamy: Pearl Harbor and its Aftermath*. New York: Doubleday, 1982.

US Congress. *Report of the Joint Committee on the Investigation of the Pearl Harbor Attack*. (Reissued by Laguna Hills, CA: Aegean Park Press, 1994.)

van der Vat, Dan. *The Pacific Campaign. The U.S.-Japanese Naval War 1941–1945*. New York: Simon & Schuster, 1991.

Warner, Peggy and Sadao Seno. *The Coffin Boats: Japanese Midget Submarine Operations in the Second World War*. London: Leo Cooper in association with Secker and Warburg, 1986.

Young, Stephen Bower. *Trapped at Pearl Harbor: Escape from Battleship Oklahoma*. New York: North River Press, and Annapolis, MD: Naval Institute Press, 1991.

Websites

There are many websites that provide information about Pearl Harbor — far too many to list here. However, two very comprehensive sites that also include relevant links are:

Pearl Harbor: Remembered
www.execpc.com/~dschaaf/mainmenu.html

USS Arizona Memorial
www.nps.gov/usar/index.html

Picture Credits

✪

Every effort has been made to correctly attribute all material reproduced in this book. If any errors have unwittingly occurred, we will be happy to correct them in future editions.

All paintings, unless otherwise designated, are by Tom Freeman © 2001. All color photographs, unless otherwise designated, are by Peter Christopher © 2001.
All maps, unless otherwise designated, are by Jack McMaster.

NA — National Archives
NH — Naval Historical Center
Goldstein — Courtesy of Donald M. Goldstein
NAM — Courtesy of US Naval Academy
    Museum/Dick Bond

Back cover: NA 80-G-36822
1   NAM
6–7 Corbis/Magma
8   Goldstein
12   (insets) (top) Courtesy of Elizabeth Mortensen; (bottom) NH 71039
12–13 NA 80-G-32741
14   (top) Bridgeman Art Library;
    (bottom left) NH 47671-KN;
    (bottom right) Mary Evans Picture Library

CHAPTER ONE

19   NA 80-G-182874
20   (top) Imperial War Museum MH 8050;
    (bottom) Imperial War Museum HU 2059
21   NH 63430
22   (top left) NA 80-G-427153;
    (middle left) NA 80-G-248975;
    (bottom left) NA 80-G-345605;
    (top right) David Craig;
    (bottom right) United States Air Force Art Collection
24   (top) NA 342-FH-3B25059;
    (bottom left) Bettmann/Corbis/Magma;
    (bottom right) Corbis/Magma
25   (top and bottom) Bettmann/Corbis/
    Magma; (middle) Brown Brothers
26   (left) Naval Security Group;
    (right) NH 225341
27   (top) Courtesy of Commander Suzuki;
    (bottom) NH 75857
28   (top) Courtesy of Raymond Brittain;
    (bottom left) Corbis/Magma;
    (top right) Courtesy of Vaughan Public Library;
    (bottom right) Courtesy of Jerry Harrington
29   (period photos) Courtesy of Charles Durham

30   (top right) Brown Brothers;
    (middle right) Courtesy of Jerry Harrington;
    (bottom right) NA SC-126867
32   (right) NA SC-99940
33   (left, middle) Bettmann/Corbis/ Magma;
    (left, bottom) NA SC-99941;
    (bottom right) Everett Collection
34   (top left) NA 342-FH-3A40793

CHAPTER TWO

36–37 NA
38   (top) Brown Brothers;
    (bottom) Corbis/Magma
39   UPI-Corbis/Bettmann/Magma
40–42 Goldstein
43   US Naval Institute
44   Corbis/Magma
45   (top and middle) Goldstein

CHAPTER THREE

50   (bottom left) NH 77079;
    (bottom right) NA 80-G-456336
53   NA 80-G-182873
54   (bottom left) NA 19-N-13752;
    (bottom right) NA 19-N-24615
55   Nimitz Museum
56   (left) NA 80-G-182259;
    (inset) NA 80-G-71198
57   NA 80-G-182249; (inset) Goldstein
58   (inset) NH 50603
58–59 Goldstein
59   (top right) Courtesy of Haruo Yoshino
60   NA 80-G-345605
61   (top) NA SC-233378;
    (bottom) NA SC-244756

CHAPTER FOUR

68   NA 80-G-32837
70   (insets) (bottom left) NA 80-G-32828;
    (bottom right) NA 80-G-32836
70–71 NA 80-G-32831
71   (right) Courtesy of Peter Nottage
72   NH 95448
73   NA 80-G-19948
75   NA 80-G-32744
76   (inset) NA
77   (top) NA; (middle) NH 51529;
    (bottom) NA 208-N-40849-PME

CHAPTER FIVE

78–79 NA 80-G-32953
81   NA 80-G-266626
82   (inset) US Naval Institute

84   (top) NA 80-G-32742;
    (middle and bottom) Courtesy of Lee Soucy
85   Courtesy of Charles Durham
86   (left) Courtesy of Yuji Akamatsu;
    (top right) NH 95812;
    (bottom right) NA 19-N-25593
87   NA 80-G-32537
88–89 Brown Brothers
90–91 NA 342-FH-3441283
90   (inset)(left) Brown Brothers
91   (inset) Brown Brothers
92   NA SC-127014
93   NA 342-FH-3A41296
94   NA 80-G-30555
95   NA SC-126996

CHAPTER SIX

96   NA 80-G-30553
97   NA
100 NH 83065
101 Courtesy of *Arizona* Memorial
104 Corbis/Magma
105 NA
106 (left) Courtesy of Edward Johann;
    (top right) NH 75840; (bottom right) Courtesy of *Arizona* Memorial
107 (top) NH 64480;
    (bottom) courtesy of John Rauschkolb
108–109 NH 64477
108 (inset) NA 80-G-33032
109 (right) Courtesy of Eugene Merrill
110 (top left) NH 62656;
    (bottom left) NA 208-PMP-68;
    (right) NH 56151
111 NA 80-G-32947
112 Courtesy of John McGoran
113 Corbis/Bettmann-UPI/Magma
114–115 NA
116–117 NA

CHAPTER SEVEN

118 80-G-32543
119 80-G-32791
120 (left) Brown Brothers;
    (top right) NA SC-242904;
    (bottom right) Courtesy of Lee Soucy
121 (top) Brown Brothers;
    (bottom left and right) Corbis/Magma
122 (top left) Courtesy of Martin Jacobs;
    (bottom left) NA 208-N-5203;
    (right) NA 80-G-32840
123 Goldstein
124 (left) Courtesy of Armand Petriccione;
    (top right) NA 80-G-266628

125 (top) NA 342-FH-3B29481;
    (bottom) NA 342-FH-3B29486
127 Courtesy of Philip Rasmussen
128 (left) NAM
129 NA 80-G-16871
130 (top) NA 80-G-32443;
    (middle) NA 80-G-32445;
    (bottom) NH 64484
131 NA
132 (top) David Craig;
    (bottom left) Corbis/Magma;
    (bottom right) NA 80-G-17079
133 (left) NAM; (below) Nimitz Museum;
    (bottom) NH 86338 KN

CHAPTER EIGHT

136–139 Goldstein
140 NH 92470
141 (left, top) Mainichi newspaper, Tokyo;
    (left, middle) NH 91772;
    (bottom left) NA SC-249636;
    (bottom right) NA SC-265357;
    (right) NH 73223
142 Corbis/Magma
143 (top) Corbis/Magma;
    (bottom left) NA 208-PU-172-H9;
    (bottom right) Courtesy of FDR Library
144 Courtesy of Celeste and Albert Brauer
145 Courtesy of Muriel Williams
146 (left) Courtesy of James Shigeru Wada;
    (top right) Brown Brothers;
    (bottom right) Corbis/Magma
147 (middle, top) Brown Brothers;
    (middle, bottom and far right) Corbis/Magma
148 (left) Courtesy of George DeLong;
    (right) NA 80-G-K-570
149 (top) NA 80-G-410534;
    (bottom left) NA 80-G-41621;
    (bottom right) NA 80-G-276818
150 NA SC-290001
151 NA 80-G-K-13871
152 (top) NH 53425;
    (bottom left) NA 80-G-7392;
    (bottom right) NA 80-G-79987-28
153 (top) NH; (bottom) NH C-4627
154–155 Courtesy of Martin Jacobs
156 Everett Collection
157 (left) NA 226-FPL-P-71,
    Robert J. Cressman Collection;
    (right) Everett Collection
169 Corbis/Magma

Index

Acknowledgments

✪

The attack on Pearl Harbor in 1941 remains as controversial as ever — one reason why it has never ceased to generate books, television programs, and motion pictures. The quantity of raw material available on the Internet verges on the terrifying. Those interested in detail, whether historians or general readers, will find Gordon W. Prange's *At Dawn We Slept* and Walter Lord's *Day of Infamy* invaluable guides (see Bibliography), as I did. Both books draw heavily on hundreds of eyewitness accounts which the passage of time has made it impossible to duplicate, let alone overhaul. I should like to acknowledge my debt to these and other predecessors.

I am no less grateful for help in locating primary material to the staffs of the US National Archives; the US Naval Historical Center in Washington, DC (especially Kathy Lloyd, Gina Akers, and Mike Walker); the USS *Arizona* Memorial at Pearl Harbor (especially Dan Martinez). In Hawaii, John Treiber patiently showed me around, introduced me to the beauty of Oahu, and dealt efficiently with a succession of follow-up queries.

I should also like to thank Mike Shaw, my literary agent, and Jonathan Pegg, his assistant, at Curtis Brown; at Madison Press Books, Ian Coutts, my editor, for his enthusiasm, patience, and attention to detail, and Al Cummings (president) and Hugh Brewster (publisher), for encouragement and hospitality; and John Lundstrom in Milwaukee for valuable pointers.

To the best of my knowledge and belief, all quoted material in this account is in the public domain. If I have inadvertently infringed on anyone's copyright, I would welcome the chance to correct matters in any future edition. The responsibility for any error or omission in the text is mine alone.

— *Dan van der Vat*

Madison Press Books would like to acknowledge and thank the following for their invaluable help during the course of this project: Daniel Martinez, historian at the USS *Arizona* Memorial, and chief ranger Dan Hand; Agnes Tauyan of Navy Public Affairs at Pearl Harbor; James Cheevers, senior curator of the United States Naval Academy Museum, and photographer Dick Bond; Jeff Hunt of the Admiral Nimitz National Museum of the Pacific War; Dawn Stitzel at the United States Naval Institute; Desoto Brown and Ron Schaeffer at the Bishop Museum in Hawaii; Christopher Geiselmann at the Curtiss Museum, Hammondsport, New York; Jan Davis, University of Arizona Library; and Junko Taguchi, who interviewed the Japanese veterans.

Special thanks to John Treiber, for tracking down survivors and photos, and helping in myriad other ways; to Jim Parker of Double Delta Industries Inc., for his excellent research in the National Archives picture collection, and for the exceptional quality of his prints; to Alex Macensky at the Naval Historical Center, for his patience and rapid turnaround of image requests; to Rick Archbold, for his invaluable work on the features; and to Professor Donald M. Goldstein, Jerry Harrington, and Martin Jacobs, for so generously sharing their respective collections with us.

We are particularly indebted to the Pearl Harbor Survivors Association, especially Bob Watson, editor of the *Gram* newsletter, and national secretary Julius A. Finnern, for their help in contacting so many Pearl Harbor survivors.

Deserving of special mention is artist Tom Freeman, whose dramatic paintings have added immensely to this book — as have his contacts among the survivors of Pearl Harbor. Thanks as well to artists Jack McMaster, for his informative maps, and David Craig.

We are also grateful to the following Pearl Harbor survivors and their families for sharing their memories and precious artifacts: Albert and Celeste Brauer; Raymond Brittain; Ruth Allison Coates; Kenneth R. Creese; George and Jeanne DeLong; Jess Dennis; Clarence Durham; Lewis D. Ellenburg; Elmer and Vicki Grayson; William Hughes; Edward A. Johann; William R. Lefabvre Sr.; John H. McGoran; B. Eugene "Gene" Merrill; George M. Mooney; Elizabeth Mortensen, the late Adolph Mortensen, and Carl Mortensen; Peter Nottage; Armand Petriccione; Philip Rasmussen; John Rauschkolb; Donald S. Sjoblom; David Smith; Lee and Margaret Soucy; and Muriel Williams.

EDITORIAL DIRECTOR
Hugh M. Brewster

✪

ASSOCIATE EDITORIAL DIRECTOR
Wanda Nowakowska

✪

PROJECT EDITOR
Ian R. Coutts

✪

ASSISTING EDITOR
Catherine Fraccaro

✪

FEATURES EDITOR
Rick Archbold

✪

ADDITIONAL EDITORIAL ASSISTANCE
Nan Froman, Susan Aihoshi

✪

PHOTO AND HISTORICAL RESEARCH
John Treiber

✪

BOOK DESIGN
Gordon Sibley Design Inc.

✪

MAP ILLUSTRATION
Jack McMaster

✪

PRODUCTION DIRECTOR
Susan Barrable

✪

PRODUCTION MANAGER
Donna Chong

✪

COLOR SEPARATION
Colour Technologies

✪

PRINTING AND BINDING
Oceanic Graphic Printing

PEARL HARBOR
THE DAY OF INFAMY — AN ILLUSTRATED HISTORY
was produced by
Madison Press Books,
which is under the direction of
Albert E. Cummings